GOD ENOUGH

KASEY LOWERY EWING

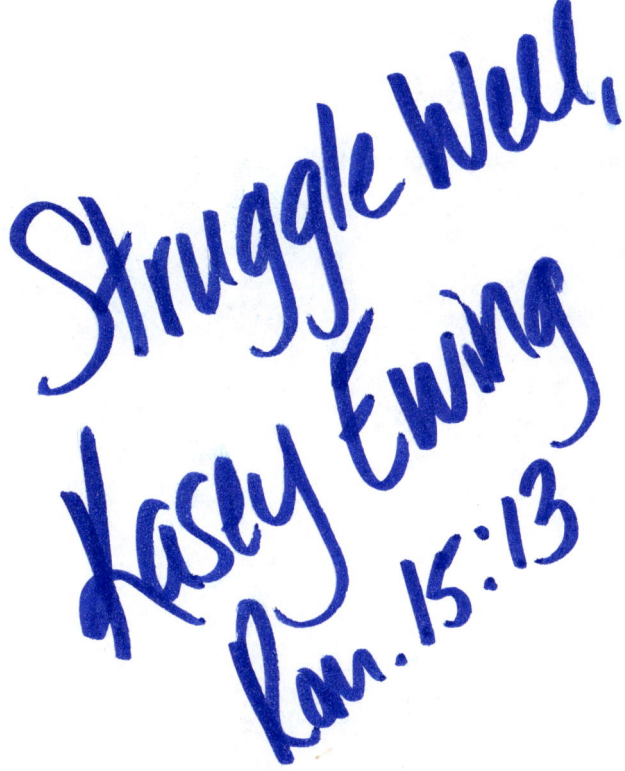

Struggle Well,
Kasey Ewing
Rom. 15:13

WWW.KASEYEWING.COM

GOD ENOUGH
Kasey Lowery Ewing

Copyright © 2011 by BJE Publishing, LLC

All rights reserved under International Copyright Law. No portion of this book may reproduced, stored in a retrieval system, or transmitted in any form or by any means - electronic, mechanical, photocopy, recording, or other - except for brief quotations in printed reviews, without prior permission of the publisher.

Contact Kasey Ewing at her website for requests to use parts of this book in the above ways.

Cover Design by Brad Ewing
Layout assistance by Sean Gregory
Stock photos from istockphoto and Shutterstock

THANK YOU...

There are so many people who made this book possible and I realize how incredibly blessed I am with the family and friends in my life.

Jen Gregory- My editor who helped me write better and kept me on track. You are the best. Thanks to Sean Gregory for helping with the layout of book cover.

Bonnie Cox, Penny Lowery (Kasey's mom) and Karen Farrar (Kasey's mother-in-law) - Spent hours editing. Thank you for the hard work!

Biggest cheerleaders who kept me going when I didn't want to anymore and encouraged me when I wanted to quit - Brandy Sexton, Dawn Coker, Kelli Taylor, Krystal Burns, Melanie Fronterhouse, Lindsay Winton, Janean Sharp, and Deb Douglas. I know I'm probably forgetting people, but please know I'm grateful.

Ginger Morrow - This book is in part a result of your mentoring over the years. There are no words to do justice to your impact in my life.

My man - Brad - by far the reason this book is finished. He kept on me when I couldn't write any more - sent me away so I could write alone and edited over and over again. You are my favorite and always will be!

My whole family - I would not have made it through many days without the prayer, love and support of my family.

My parents and my sisters - Charles and Penny Lowery, Angela Cunningham and Breanne Vasquez - have seen me through so many battles. We have persevered through much!

My boys - Drew, Jake and Jackson - I love you so much!

4TABLE OF CONTENTS

FOREWORD — 7
Michael Catt

INTRODUCTION — 11
Moonless Trust by Elisabeth Elliot

PREFACE — 13

CHAPTER ONE — 17
T.R.O.U.B.L.E.

CHAPTER TWO — 25
Stallions and Bad Hair

CHAPTER THREE — 32
Plan B

CHAPTER FOUR — 39
Sweet Fellowship

CHAPTER FIVE — 42
Enter My Knight

CHAPTER SIX — 47
Be Careful What You Pray For

CHAPTER SEVEN — 53
What Just Happened?

CHAPTER EIGHT — 64
The Rising Fog

CHAPTER NINE — 71
Gaining Some Perspective

CHAPTER TEN — 76
A Time For Everything

CHAPTER ELEVEN — 82

Letters Of Hope
CHAPTER TWELVE 92
It Is Well

CHAPTER THIRTEEN 102
Choosing To Worship

CHAPTER FOURTEEN 113
Uncertain

CHAPTER FIFTEEN 120
Self Preservation

CHAPTER SIXTEEN 125
He's Not Safe, But He's Good

CHAPTER SEVENTEEN 130
Waiting And Blessings

CHAPTER EIGHTEEN 140
Introducing Job

CHAPTER NINETEEN 145
Struggle Well

CHAPTER TWENTY 150
Walls

CHAPTER TWENTY ONE 154
Why Vs. Who

CHAPTER TWENTY TWO 163
The Power Of The Word

CHAPTER TWENTY THREE 166
Back To Life. Back To
Reality

CHAPTER TWENTY FOUR 174
Mountain Hikes And Pressing On

APPENDIX ONE 183

Survival Playlists

APPENDIX TWO   **185**
Journal Entries

APPENDIX THREE   **201**
Thoughts From A Close Friend, Krystal Burns

TO THE READER   **217**
A gift for our readers

FOREWORD

Michael Catt
Senior Pastor, Sherwood Baptist Church in Albany, GA
Executive Producer, Sherwood Pictures

In 1973 as Sara Havner, the wife of Vance Havner, lay dying of a fatal and dreaded disease, she wrote, "I have had to endure many things that I cannot tell you...until..." She died soon after. Following her death, Vance Havner wrote a classic on suffering and dying entitled *Though I Walk Through the Valley*. It was his bestselling book because, at some point, all of us walk through that valley.

When a loved one is gone, we are driven to remember that God is not gone. His love for us is not gone. His grace is not gone. William Jennings Bryan said, "Christ has made of death a narrow, starlit strip between companionships of yesterday and the reunions of tomorrow."

This is a story of a loved one gone, but not forgotten. It's told by a young woman I have known since she was a baby. She was that little girl that could steal your heart and make you laugh…and that caused her parents' prayer life to increase. Kasey was a pistol. That fiery young girl who has become a godly woman is one of my favorite people on the planet.

They say no two people are alike. I believe when God made Kasey, He gave her a personality and a resolve that has served her well. God, being sovereign, knew the tests, trials, and temptations she would face along life's road. He gave her a tenacity that has, by His grace, been pruned and is bearing fruit. Part of that fruit is the book you hold in your hands today.

Kasey is a "God-honest" person. This is something strangely lacking in the church today. She speaks with the voice of a prophet. She is a no-nonsense person and yet has a bubbling personality. I guess I love the prophet side of Kasey because, as a prophet myself, I like her pull-no-punches, take-no-prisoners style. But like Jeremiah, she is a weeping prophet. Pain has tempered her. Grace has shaped her. God's love has sustained her.

I'm weary of reading books with pat answers written by people who aren't honest enough to admit they even have questions. American Christians have, for too long, been drinking the Kool-Aid of the Prosperity gospel. We need authors and speakers like Kasey.

Kasey brings to us a biblical approach to sorrow and suffering. She is more honest about these matters than the majority of preachers on television today. She is also closer to a true interpretation of life and of the Scriptures. She and her family have walked through the valley, but have chosen not to hide in a cave.

Kasey reminds me of the spirit of the Psalmist. He didn't hide his feelings, anger, uncertainty, confusion, or pain. He poured it out to God. The Psalms remind us that we can be honest and not threaten God's sovereignty or His love for us. Kasey's testimony is a reminder of the great grace of our God.

This book represents an honest approach to life and death, to being overcome and overcoming. Kasey has done what many pastors fail to do in times of grief. She's been honest. She's faced the emotions head-on. She hasn't fallen for catch phrases and Christian slogans. And Kasey isn't merely a survivor. No, she's an overcomer. There is no "pie in the sky" theology here. Just honest, forthright confession of the struggles of a mom, dad, husband, and wife going through a horrific tragedy.

I'm grateful Kasey wrote this. I'm honored to write the forward. The pain of writing your own story is offset by the knowledge that somewhere, someone has faced a similar crisis and has no one who understands. Kasey and her family have "been there." Consider this book a grace gift. If it has found its way into your hands, you can pause and thank God for a beautiful young mother and wife who had the courage to say, "You aren't alone."

INTRODUCTION

Some of you are perhaps feeling that you are voyaging just now on a moonless sea. Uncertainty surrounds you. There seem to be no signs to follow. Perhaps you feel about to be engulfed by loneliness. There is no one to whom you can speak of your need.

Amy Carmichael wrote of such a feeling when, as a missionary of twenty-six, she had to leave Japan because of poor health, then travel to China for recuperation, but then realized God was telling her to go to Ceylon. (All this preceded her going to India, where she stayed for fifty-three years.) I have on my desk her original handwritten letter of August 25, 1894, as she was en route to Colombo. "All along, let us remember, we are not asked to understand, but simply to obey.... On July 28, Saturday, I sailed. We had to come on board on Friday night, and just as the tender (a small boat) where were the dear friends who had come to say goodbye was moving off, and the chill of loneliness shivered through me, like a warm love-clasp came the long-loved lines–'And only Heaven is better than to walk with Christ at midnight, over moonless seas.' I couldn't feel frightened then. Praise Him for the moonless seas–all the better the opportunity for proving Him to be indeed the El Shaddai, 'the God who is Enough.'"

Let me add my own word of witness to hers and to that of the tens of thousands who have learned that He is indeed Enough. He is not all we would ask for (if we were honest), but it is precisely when we do not have what we would ask for, and only then, that we can clearly perceive His all-sufficiency. It is when the sea is moonless that the Lord has become my Light.[1]

---

[1] Moonless Trust devotion from Keep a Quiet Heart By Elizabeth Elliot

PREFACE

It was a cold Colorado night, forty degrees and rapidly dropping. I was off to freeze through yet another football game, a scrimmage that I was dreading. Drew was the quarterback for a new team of boys that had never played the game.

First-time football players defending your quarterback against more experienced players is not a good thing. I was in for a night of cringing and praying that my growing boy would just keep getting up after each hit. I looked for him on the bottom of every pile and prayed that he'd still be moving.

As the scrimmage moved along, I watched in slow motion as a man-sized child came around from the back and horse-collared my son. His body dropped to the ground as the mini Hercules jumped up and down in celebration. He had sacked the quarterback.

Drew finally got up, but slowly. He motioned to me that he was fine and went back onto the field. As the game continued, he was hit over and over again. Play after play, he went to the ground. I kept thinking to myself that someone needed to stop this madness but I didn't say a word, which in hindsight is totally out of character for me.

I am usually right behind the coach offering my suggestions like Sandra Bullock in the movie *Blindside*. One of my many favorite scenes is when she calls the coach on her cell phone from the stands. Why didn't I think to do that this night?

Instead I just watched and waited. Dread filled my heart. Drew wasn't looking right. He bent down to take the snap, stood straight up, walked off the field, and fell to the ground.

By the time I got to him, he was moving in and out of consciousness, and he couldn't feel his right side. Someone told me later that I kept saying over and over, "You can't do this to me again. You can't do this to me again!" This was not the first time I had watched one of my children move in and out of consciousness.

As I knelt down over Drew sprawled out on prickly green turf there was an all too familiar terror growing deep within. I prayed and told God "NO!" Riding to the hospital, I turned my head to the back to watch the paramedic work on Drew as we sped away from the field.

I fumbled with my cell phone trying to call Brad but my legs and arms were shaking and I couldn't dial the right number. I watched as they pricked Drew with a needle as long as a ruler.

The paramedics were stabbing him up and down his arms and legs numerous times trying to get his body to respond to the needle. Nothing.

He could not feel the needle, and all I could feel was the tension and the numerous shakes my own body couldn't control. He felt nothing, and I was feeling everything.

I could barely see the top of Drew's head. All I could see was his blond hair spilling out over the white bed sheet. I just kept telling the Lord, "I can't do this again. I can't Lord. Please don't make me. Just please let him be okay."

As I rode in that ambulance, my mind was going places it shouldn't go. I mentally weighed which results I could and could not handle. If he was paralyzed, I could handle that. If he was brain damaged, I could handle that. I could handle anything if God would just let him live. In the fear and terror of the moment, I was giving God His options.

After Drew's initial tests in Colorado Springs, the doctors decided to airlift him to Denver. After a long night and many tests later, it was determined that he had sustained a severe concussion. The mental horror had been lowered to mild panic, and I was starting to breathe normally for the first time in several hours. As the dark night unfolded, I sat in the molded plastic chair lulled by the steady beeps and hums of equipment and began to process what had happened. Quiet tears tugged at the corners of my eyes.

Why is it that on one trip to the hospital, I left empty handed and another I walked out with my life still intact? I was staring at Drew but my heart was gazing at the past asking the same questions we all ask at some point. Why Lord? Why, me? Why, us?

CHAPTER ONE
T.R.O.U.B.L.E.

I'm sure it's a question my parents asked a time or two, "Why Lord? Why us?" I was mischievous from day one. I was the kid that made others parents sigh in relief because they didn't have to raise me. My uncle once told me, "If you weren't so cute, I would kill you."

I needed all of that personality to get me out of all the trouble I seemed to find myself in. Once, I told a nursery worker that if she didn't get down on her knees and play with me under the table I was going to have her fired. I was a third generation preachers kid and had the audacity to think that everyone in the church should do what I said.

I got the nickname of "fireball" fairly quickly. I was full of energy - a daredevil, a fighter. I knew what I wanted and went after it. I was hell on wheels and didn't slow down for much. I took so many trips to the emergency room that we used to laugh that I had my own ER doctor.

I often wonder why my parents didn't just lock me in a padded cell and throw away the key. As I grew older, my playful shenanigans turned into teenage drama. I thought the world owed me something, and I was hell bent to figure out what it was.

There was a dangerous sparkle in my blue eyes that said I was ready to take on the world, one high school cheerleader at a time. I was caring and fun loving yet not totally sure of my place in the world. I struggled between my church life and my school world, and they never seemed to mesh together.

I remember the exact minute that my heart changed. I was in photography class my sophomore year of high school. Right there in the center of class, surrounded by teachers, students and photography equipment, I decided that I had had enough and that I would no longer be subjected to the goody-two-shoes pastor's daughter label I had worked so hard to gain.

I didn't want it anymore - I wanted attention but not that kind. I was sitting there contemplating how I wanted to be seen. The good girl was wearing thin, the constant teasing and attention were wearing me down. I began to rewrite my story. I wish I could explain why.

I began to listen to other voices, give in to small changes, seek peoples affirmation of who I wanted to be, and not who Jesus wanted me to be. This gradual shift quieted the small voice telling me how to live. It loudly objected at first, but the longer I ignored it, the quieter it got until the voice became barely a whisper that I no longer cared to hear.

It was the worst decision I could have made. It was a decision to stop following God and taste what I thought was a life of freedom. I decided that day in photography class that my parents and God didn't know what was best and I did. My small decisions lead to larger decisions which resulted in a life of habitual sin. It was a heart change that led to heartbreak.

Every time I read through Exodus, I think about Pharaoh. I often sigh to myself, "What an idiot!" But I was just like Pharaoh, especially in my teenage years. I knew of God. I grew up in a Christian home. My dad was a pastor, for heaven's sake! I had some good "Moses-like" people in my life trying to show me that I needed to obey God. I would repent briefly; then just like Pharaoh, when the plague of disobedience was lifted, my heart would harden.[2]

I wanted relief from my troubles, but I did not want a Lord for my life. Once after Moses had calmed the plague of thunder and hail he said, "I will stop the thunder and hail, so you may know that the earth is the Lord's. But I know that you and

---
[2] Exodus 8: 15

your officials still do not fear the Lord God." [3] That was me. I didn't fear the Lord, I just feared consequences.

I remember one night, sleeping in my car, too scared to go home after partying too hard. I had nowhere to go. Leaning back the seat of my white sports car, I pleaded with God to help me. I fitfully slept on and off, desperately waiting for daylight to come, for light in the darkness.

Dawn appeared, I drove home and quietly tried to sneak into my house hoping I wouldn't be heard. My Dad was sitting in his big leather chair, waiting on me. He had been up all night. With red, sorrowful eyes he asked where I had been. I was instantly ashamed and sorry I had hurt him and caused him fear. I begged my dad's forgiveness, but only for the night.

Just like Pharaoh, another plague would hit and I was crying out again, "I have sinned against the Lord your God and against you. Now forgive my sin once more and pray to the Lord your God to take this deadly plague away from me."[4]

This isn't true repentance. It's a cry to stop the pain, and I lived this way for years. I don't tell you this to celebrate my

---

[3] Exodus 9:29b-30

[4] Exodus 10:16-17

sin. I tell you so that God will get glory even from my mistakes. My prayer in writing this is that God can say, "But I will gain glory for myself through Pharaoh [Kasey] and all his army, and the Egyptians [people around Kasey] will know that I am the LORD." [5] If God can do all of that through me, He can do it with anyone. If the Lord can take a shamed girl and turn her into a devoted follower of Christ, He is God enough.

That day in photography class when I decided to make my own decisions, my life began to spiral out of control. That one small decision led to bigger decisions that eventually caused me to wake up one freezing January day, my freshman year in college, pregnant.

I wondered if I had gotten some kind of stomach bug that forced me to spend a whole plane ride home from Christmas break in the cramped bathroom trying to quietly throw up in a way that the whole plane didn't know I was sick. I slid down the wall of the bathroom with my knees touching the toilet, wondering how many more times I could possibly get sick. There couldn't be much more left inside of me, could there?

---
[5] Exodus 14: 5

We finally landed, and I felt a little better on the ground. I tried to eat some crackers and drink small sips of Coke. I made it to my dorm, crawled into bed, and slept through the night. I awoke the next day feeling more miserable than before. A tiny thought nagged me in the back of my mind. Something wasn't right, but I quickly pushed it aside.

I was hoping I had the stomach flu. I lay in bed for a few days, and then wondered why I didn't feel better yet. The tiny thought in the back of my head began to expand into possibilities that I didn't want to consider. My symptoms were close to the stomach flu, but I had others symptoms that had nothing to do with the flu.

After a week of the stomach flu "that wasn't," I went to the store and bought a pregnancy test. Our college was in a small town just on the outskirts of a larger town. I made sure to go into the larger town so that no one would see me purchase a pregnancy test. I slipped into my dorm room and checked to make sure my roommates were all at class. I took the test and waited for the two minute answer that would change my life forever.

I knew the answer deep down, but I needed those two lines of proof, as if the constant gagging and nausea weren't enough! Two smudgy hot pink lines quickly appeared. The truth settled in deep as I sat on the cold, grey and black tiled floor and wept.

I now know why God calls us to "above all else, guard your heart, for it is the wellspring of life[6]." Our heart tells us how to act. When I began contemplating in my heart that God's ways were not for me, my actions became consistent with what my heart believed.

God was not willing to allow me to run free; He would continue to pursue me and allow the consequences of my actions to force me to turn to Him. God has been called the 'hound of heaven', and I joke that I still have scars on my ankles where He was nipping at me to repent and turn around.

It is His kindness that leads us to repentance. God's allowing us to suffer is, in fact, His kindness. He is so thoughtful that He continues to hound us to draw us to Him and away from sin. Read that last sentence again so that it sinks in.

---

[6] Proverbs 4:23

In the Old Testament, He consistently brings challenges and war to the Israelites so that they will be forced to come to Him for guidance and help. His best end result for us is a heart turned towards Him, acknowledging we need His help.

The minute we step out of His boundaries, God begins to act on our behalf. God allows consequences and events to rock our world simply to bring us toward Him. It is His deep love for us that allows us to "get caught." God so often shows us in His dealings with Israel that He wants to reign over our lives and He is willing to cause and allow events so that we listen to Him. His judgment on us is to turn us back to Him. His discipline towards us is to move us in a direction towards Him and Him alone. He causes me to love Him, He creates a need in me so deep that only He can fill... I can't help but love that today.

CHAPTER TWO
STALLIONS AND BAD HAIR

There is nothing like being a pregnant teen to let the world know you have been up to no good. There is no hiding it - I had hidden many things, and now God was calling my bluff. No more pretending. Choices were going to have to be made. What would I do?

Would I continue to allow my ways to control my actions or would I finally give up completely and let God rule my life? God forced my hand, you could say. Through the consequences of my own actions, I was finally willing to fold and allow Him to work.

The second book of Corinthians, chapter three, verse three says, "You show that you are a letter from Christ, the result of our ministry, written not with ink but with the Spirit of the living God, not on tablets of stone but on tablets of human hearts." I finally gave Him something to write on - My heart.

I began to listen to His voice again. I no longer wanted relief from my pain, I wanted Him. Blinders were being removed from my eyes and I was truly starting to see God. Not just a God of rules and regulations but a God who really loved me.

I struggled with loneliness, fear, bitterness, resentment; you name it, I felt it. Thankfully, I had really great parents. My parents had come into town for a visit, and I knew I had to break the news. My dad had rented a condo for the whole family to spend some time together.

I wanted to blurt out the news, but I was so scared. I knew that they would love me no matter what, but I also knew that my dad would get untold amounts of grief from the people in my home church that he pastored.

I wasn't just offering news that would personally hurt them, but it would also hurt his role as a pastor. I got a first hand lesson on how our sins affect those around us as well.

We all arrived at the condo, unloaded our luggage, and sat around the kitchen. My mom immediately began organizing the kitchen. I sat down at the brown, round kitchen table, and I quickly blurted out, "I have something to tell you, I am pregnant." I watched my mom's face fall, fear quickly rising in her eyes and hurt washing over her. My dad just stood there, trying to get his emotions under control before he spoke. Under his breath I heard, "I should have killed that boy last summer."

He hugged me, told me he loved me, and would support me no matter what.

He asked me if I was going to get married, "NO!" I shouted, scared that was what they wanted. I knew that I didn't want to complicate a pregnancy with a premature marriage. It is strange to me that I knew that I didn't want to marry the father, but I hadn't had enough sense to stay away from him until now.

I instinctively knew I didn't want to spend the rest of my life with him, yet I allowed him into places I should have guarded. I was adamant that I wanted to do this alone. They both promised to support me no matter what, and I was relieved that they didn't want me to get married just because I was pregnant.

I had to move out of my dorm. I'm sure that a pregnant teenager on a Baptist college campus doesn't send the "right message" to prospective students. I realized it was part of the consequences of my bad choices. I moved into a one bedroom apartment close to family and friends.

Some days the magnitude of what I had done would send me hiding into my room. I was very sick in my early stages of pregnancy and spent many mornings throwing up and lying on the cold bathroom floor. I would lie there, begging for relief from the nausea. I couldn't believe what was happening to me.

It is one thing to see two pink lines on a stick but this harsh new reality washed over me every time I felt a wave of nausea. How could I have been so selfish? I had brought harm and grief to my whole family, yet, they loved me and stood beside me anyway.

I have often heard that the way we see our heavenly Father has a lot to do with how we see our earthly father. I can see that it was easy to accept and understand God's love and forgiveness for me because my own father displayed that type of love and forgiveness each and every time I disappointed him. I was beyond blessed to have a dad that showed me a grace through my pregnancy that allowed me to accept the same grace from my God.

To have been a teenager who often used my figure and charm to get my way, pregnancy sure cured that. One day, I went to the gas station and left crying simply because I saw my reflection in the doorway. I was no longer a cute sized two teenager. I was six months pregnant, and I couldn't even recognize myself. My brother-in-law told me I looked like "an olive on tooth picks."

I was feeling particularly vulnerable and just plain ugly so I decided to visit the beauty salon and get a new "do". Only it didn't turn out the way I wanted. I was going for the Meg Ryan look back when she was cute and her hair stuck up all over.

Now I not only looked like an olive, I looked like an olive impersonating Elvis. It was awful. I was nineteen, pregnant, very round, and now I had horrible hair. The hair almost put me over the edge. I had already lost my reputation, my youth, my figure, and now I had the worst hairdo ever!

It felt like I had lost everything. God intervened on my behalf and taught me a lesson then that I hope to never forget. He stripped away everything that I held dear to or relied on for my security but HIM.

Recently, I was with my cousin Christy, who happens to be one of my best friends. She was diagnosed with breast cancer not too long ago. One afternoon, we were hanging out on her back porch as her husband began shaving her head due to the chemo. I watched as the hair fell to the ground and remembered the day I felt like God shaved me of everything I held on to. I watched as God did the same thing for my Christy.

I watched her grasp the beauty of who she was in God. I watched as she was transformed from the inside out. I watched as she realized in that exact moment that God was enough. He was all she needed. She didn't need anything but Him. It was one of the most beautiful things I have witnessed!

I was honored to stand there while she was transformed into a woman radiating His love inside of her. She was the most gorgeous woman I have ever seen at that moment. I was speechless. I watched as God gave her a precious gift. He showed her that no matter what we encounter in this life, He is enough!

As I sit here writing, I am at my parents house in the country. They are surrounded by horses. I can't help but think that I was like a wild stallion that needed breaking. God was going to keep at it until I relented and allowed Him control over my life. I needed to submit.

To a stallion, submitting feels like failure, like giving up who you are. You're so afraid that an effort to obey God will kill everything wild and wonderful. You find it hard to trust, so you buck. God knows that a wild stallion has the potential not only to be a powerful and beautiful species but a purposeful and useful species as well.

When we are controlled by a rider who knows the path ahead, who can steer us and guide us, we become an entirely new species; a truly wild and wonderful species of His own making. I am so thankful that God is faithful to teach me the hard lessons even when it hurts. Little did I know that the stripping of everything I held dear to me would later prepare me for the greatest loss I have ever experienced.

CHAPTER THREE
PLAN B

As my pregnancy progressed, I was very much still that same old wild stallion. I felt like I had the perfect plan in place. Adoption would be the answer to my immediate problem. After weeks of sifting through parent profiles, I picked out the perfect family. My own family was supportive and willing to walk me through the process. My mom spent most of my pregnancy with me. Everyone loved on me and supported me. In the days leading up to delivery, I was content with the decision to give my baby up for adoption. I felt that it was the good and right decision.

Two weeks before my due date, my mom had to go home for the weekend to a church dinner. (Don't you just know that I was the topic of many conversations at that church dinner! Nothing like your pastor's unwed pregnant daughter to keep the chit chat fresh.) My cousin, Christy, who had been with me the whole time too, was headed home for a quick weekend with her family.

I spent the weekend watching movies and waiting on this nightmare to be over. I was relieved that soon I could get back to my normal life, put my past behind me, and move on.

I was contemplating what I wanted to do after I had the baby. I knew things would never be the same again. I was nineteen and felt I had already lived a lifetime. The carefree, do what you want days were over. My life was going to look different. I would forever be changed and scarred by the last nine months.

My former life was unrecognizable. I was beginning to see glimpses of the new creation, the new species, that God was creating in me. Yet, I was still desperate. Desperate to fit into a college world that had no place for a pregnant teen. Desperate to begin a new chapter in my life where lawyers and OB-GYN were not the people I talked to on a daily basis.

I knew God was going to use this time in my life and that He was writing a new story for me, but I was overly eager to see some fruit from the hardship.

It had been an uneventful day. I watched French Kiss for the hundredth time. Meg Ryan eased my heartache with her own fairy tale heartbreak even if she was the catalyst for that horrible hair do!

I laughed as she followed her ex-boyfriend around France trying to win him back. The make believe and happy ending gave me hope that the mess I had made of my life would result in its own happy ending. I ate take out and hid in my apartment. This "olive on toothpicks" didn't want to be seen by anyone, so I holed up in my living room with my television to keep me company.

I thought about getting up and going to my room to sleep but I didn't want to fall asleep alone. I stayed on the couch hoping the people on the screen would drown out the loneliness I felt inside. Darkness started to creep in the windows, and I steeled myself for one more night till my mom came back to be with me.

That's when I began to feel a sharp pain in my back. Then I felt it again. I opened my pregnancy book. Maybe a contraction? I had no idea. The book suggested a bath. Alone and scared, I got in the bathtub in my one bedroom apartment. I wasn't sure what was happening to me. It hurt, but then it went away. I kept reading and learning how to time contractions. I was about to have a baby. Alone.

A friend took me to the hospital. I checked myself in and laid in the bed crying out in agony. I have never felt such pain and loneliness in my entire life. I could see out of the window from my bed, and I remember thinking how dark and scary it was out there. Everything felt that way.

This was not how it was supposed to have happened. Life was not turning out the way I had dreamed it would! I didn't call my parents or my cousin. It was late at night; they couldn't make it anyway. I thought to myself, "You got yourself into this, handle it!" I relished the sheer pain of it, feeling the weight of my punishment. I kept telling myself, "Just do what you need to do."

I wish I could tell you that I cried out to God, that He sustained me, and that I prayed all night for this baby. I did none of that. I cried out in sheer pain and misery. I knew God was there, but for the night, I felt He didn't want anything to do with me and that I was getting my well deserved spanking.

Remembering all of the pain and aloneness and all of the shame and heartbreak, I think of Jesus. Remembering those feelings gives me a tiny, tiny glimpse of the magnitude of what Jesus did on the cross. As I recall how my body heaved with contractions, the shame that filled my inmost being, and my sin heaped on me, I am left thankful to Jesus. I am very aware that there is no way to fully grasp all that Jesus did for me.

The pain and shame radiating through my body forced screams of agony. Jesus willingly got on the cross and felt the shame and sin of the whole world. It felt like too much for me to bear, yet He endured it all. For me. As I lay there in a dim hospital room, I wondered if I would ever recover.

Relief from the physical pain was given through an IV, and I endured the night. If only the relief had come so easily for the mental torture I was fighting in my head. I finally delivered a healthy baby boy in the wee hours of the morning with not one single family member or friend by my side. However, things did not go according to my plan.

Why I ever had any confidence that my plan would work out is a mystery. I certainly should have been used to the fact that my plans did not work by now. I think I was a bit numb to the reality of what was truly going on.

My doctor wasn't there, my family wasn't there, and somehow my chart did not indicate that I was giving the baby up for adoption. The nurse handed me the smallest, reddest faced baby I had ever seen. He was wrapped up so tight and looked like a tiny football. She laid him in my arms, and I held him. He snuggled up close to me and relaxed totally in my arms.

He was mine, and I wasn't letting go.

Lying in that hospital bed, holding my new born baby, something changed. Once I felt his weight in my arms, how could I ever let him go? A wave of something I didn't understand was rising up in me. A mother's love sprung up quickly and instantly. None of us had prepared for that.

I never allowed myself to feel anything for the baby because I knew I was going to give him up. I shut off any feelings of favor or attachment, knowing it would hurt to give him away, but I couldn't shut off these feelings as I lay there holding my new baby.

The stallion had felt the feel of the saddle and this time I did not resist.

In the early hours of the morning while the doctors were examining my baby, a nurse sat in my room with me and worked on her charts. I was drifting off, in and out of sleep, on a lot of pain medicine. I remember wondering if she was an angel.

I am not one to fantasize, but I knew that God was watching over me as she just sat there. She told me she was praying for me, that her husband was a pastor of a small church, and that she understood how I must feel. She stayed near me until my family got there. I was a pitiful sight, a young teenage girl, all alone in a hospital room with a new baby boy and the weight of some major decisions hanging right over me.

Family began to arrive, and the realization was dawning on them that I had changed my mind. My dad and my cousin Christy headed to Wal-mart for a car seat. I started to debate names.

I sat in the hospital holding my son, Drew, and everyone else sat around me just staring. They were wondering what to do and what on earth to say. I walked out of the hospital at nineteen years old with a new baby and no idea as to how to be a single mom in college.

CHAPTER FOUR
SWEET FELLOWSHIP

My fun loving college days turned into diapers and spit up. I was a mom in college. I went to our weekly college Bible study when Drew was an infant. He screamed most of the time, and I spent the hour hiding in the bathroom trying to get him to be quiet. I overheard someone say, "This is a Bible study not a nursery" as we were leaving. I never went back.

I was no longer a kid. I had to grow up and grow up fast. The reality of being totally responsible for another human being weighed heavy on me.

I had slowly begun going back to church. Picture a nineteen year old girl, pregnant, unwed and scared to death. She walks into a church which is hard for her to do. She grew up in church. (Her dad was a pastor, for crying out loud.) It really was the last place I wanted to be, but I knew it was where I needed to be.

Church has never seemed like a safe place to me. When you are a pastors kid, church just isn't the same. This time, I was no longer the pastor's daughter but a pregnant college girl. What a scene I must have made! I found there was a pleasant surprise, though. This particular church had a welcoming spirit, a heart for worship, and a choir that radiated joy.

At this church, I found a pastor who loved me regardless of my mistakes. I was welcomed completely by him and loved to hear him preach God's word. It felt like he was talking directly to me each week.

I also met a group of ladies. They called themselves the Lunch Bunch, they went out eat together each week after Bible study and always welcomed new women to join. I grew as I was taught to study my Bible and I was discipled by a very dear older woman and a wonderful pastor.

They supported me and gave me a place to belong. I was finally able to walk into a church where no one cared who my dad was. Most of my church experience had been people loving me when they wanted to get close to my dad or mad at me when they were mad at him.

I needed a place where I could fall in love with Jesus and learn about Him without the other baggage that comes with being a pastor's kid. I was ready for a new stage in my life, and finally I was getting grounded in God's word, not other peoples' opinions of the Bible. I was learning it for myself.

I met a kind and mature woman named Ginger who had this gorgeous silver hair that crowned her righteous life. She was the perfect picture of wisdom and grace. Her laugh was loud and enduring at the same time. I just knew looking at her that she had something I needed.

She took a liking to me and began teaching me to follow God's Word. She taught Precept Bible studies and I sat under her teaching and wrote down every word that came out of her mouth. I was so drawn to her, but I didn't know exactly why. She taught with a toughness and a tenderness that spoke directly to my heart. She challenged me, she encouraged me, and she spoke truth to me.

Her words were not always easy, but she said them with a soft tongue that pierced just the right places. Ginger showed me what a godly woman looked like. She was God's gift to me at that time in my life and continued to be as my life began to evolve. This stallion was learning that the only reason it had hurt to be led was because I was pulling so fiercely in resistance to my idea of what it meant to be tamed. Ginger was the perfect example of a tamed stallion to me. I had finally figured out what church was for, and I was hooked.

CHAPTER FIVE
ENTER MY KNIGHT

One Sunday after church, I heard laughing outside my window. I peered out to see what was going on, and I noticed him. I had met Brad before. He had been loud and obnoxious, and I was immediately turned off by how unreserved he was.

Being a single mom had made me very serious and uptight. That afternoon, he had just returned from church, and I saw a spark of something I wanted to know more about. He intrigued me. He was different from the guys I was normally drawn to. Different looked good considering the last year of my life.

I wasn't looking. I wasn't looking at all. I had determined that I could do life alone with my son and that I could bear the burden and responsibility that came with being a single mother in college.

Anything that required me to need Jesus on a daily basis felt really good. I had done it alone for so long that I wanted Jesus to be a part of everything I did. I was even scared to believe that there was someone good and right out there for me. I still didn't truly believe I deserved a happy ending.

Yet, this guy continued to pop up in my life. It seemed like every time I turned around, he was there. One day I was moving to a new apartment, and when Brad and his friend Josh happened to drive by, they helped me move my stuff to the new place. He offered friendship and help, and he cooked for me. Cook for me, and I am yours. He also teased me incessantly and forced me to see life in brighter colors.

One day he and his friend Josh offered to watch Drew for me so that I could run a few errands. I was excited to walk the grocery store aisles alone. I was so lonely before I had my baby and now I felt like I was never alone! The chance to walk up and down the isles without a crying baby is not something you resist. Peace as a young mom is walking by yourself up and down an aisle of any store.

I finished my shopping and returned to my apartment. As I pulled up to my parking spot, the front door was visible and I saw a note on my front door. I thought it was very strange because it wasn't there before, and then I began to look around and notice that Josh's truck wasn't in the spot next to mine.

Panic flooded my mind and I couldn't imagine what was wrong. What could have happened that they had to leave? I rushed to the door and barely glanced at the note that said something about them having to go somewhere. I dashed inside to find Drew playing under his red and black floor mobile, swatting at the toys hanging down. I called for Brad and Josh, but they didn't answer. I read the note again more carefully this time. It said they had to run home real quick and figured Drew would be fine for a few minutes.

    What? They left a baby home alone? I was dumbfounded. What idiots! Who would do such a thing? I called my mom and told her what had happened. While I was on the phone, I began picking up all of their stuff they had at my house and tossing it out the front door. I grabbed shirts, book bags, and anything else I could find and threw it in a pile on the front walkway. Then I heard quiet laughter. It increased until they loudly jumped out of the closet. Brad and Josh. Those goofballs were playing a joke on me! In the last couple of years, I've finally gotten to the point where I can laugh at the story without a tinge of anger rising up my neck.

    Even with the added fun and frustration of Brad and his way of living life, I was still determined to make it on my own. I continually resurrected walls of bitterness and anger towards life and relationships, but as quickly as I built them, Brad tore them down. The way He loved the Lord, his voice lifted up in praise, his tenderness with my son... I was losing my battle with independence.

Friendship quickly progressed into something more and we talked all the time and giggled and enjoyed life together. Over spring break, Brad went to Canada on a choir concert with our school. He was gone for a week, and we promptly realized after a week apart just how much we meant to each other. Now we just had to convince the world, and most importantly our parents, that we were meant to be together.

We took a weekend away and drove to Brad's house to meet his parents. I was scared to death. I was not exactly a girl parents dreamed their son would marry. I had a baby after all.

We pulled into their driveway, got Drew out of the car seat, and walked slowly to the back door. I busied myself messing with Drew's bib and clothes, looking for anything to do other than meeting his parents. We walked in, and they graciously welcomed me to their home. Brad's mom took me upstairs to the room I would be staying in and left me alone for a minute to settle in.

I shut the door, breathed a sigh of relief, and unloaded all of my stuff. I looked on the bed, and right on top of the floral bedspread was a small toy with a card on it for Drew. I let out a deep breath. That small gesture for Drew meant so much to me.

In a small way, Brad's mom was showing me that she welcomed Drew as well as me. Brad grew up for years with a single mom, so she knew just what to do to show her support for Drew and me.

After dating for a few months, we were engaged and then married. After all, I had a baby. Instant family. God worked it out so that Brad could adopt Drew right after the wedding. I was overwhelmed with God's provision for myself and my son. He quickly redeemed my situation and my heart and offered solace for a lonely, scarred single mom.

CHAPTER SIX
BE CAREFUL WHAT YOU PRAY FOR

Cue the happy ending. I was loving this story God was writing. It was so amazing to see how God had taken my mistakes and turned them into miracles. He had orchestrated the perfect love story. Movies were made out of stories like this. The godly, handsome man comes in to rescue the single mom, and they live happily ever after. My Christian version of Jerry Maguire - Brad really did complete me!

Doesn't that just sound good? Make you feel all tingly inside? God's story of redemption. I had one of those testimonies, and it was testimony time. Tell the world! Look what God has done! I made the perfect Sunday morning sermon illustration. Only God wasn't finished with our story.

Brad and I finished school and moved to Albuquerque, New Mexico to begin our lives together as a family. My dad was the pastor of a church there, and we accepted the call to join their staff. I found out I was pregnant, but this time it was a lot of fun to tell my parents. Ha!

About nine months later, I began to feel that same pressure in my back again; only now I knew I was going into labor. And I was not alone. It was a much better experience. We loaded up, dropped Drew off at my parents, and headed for the hospital. We arrived and began filling out all the forms.

I laughed at one form that I signed agreeing that we would not hold the hospital responsible if dad got hurt during labor. The nurses said we'd be surprised how many dads were injured during delivery. She joked about how many men fall and hit their heads from passing out at the sight of their wives in labor. I laughed again never thinking that we might run into the same problem.

After a long night of labor, we knew it was time. Brad was ready, I was ready. I began to push. Brad was helping, only he didn't look so good. He was a little green. Then he told my sister he needed to sit for a minute. I watched him slink to the floor and then crawl on all fours to the bathroom.

I was pushing and trying to concentrate, but I was having trouble. All I could focus on was the loudest, most obnoxious screaming and retching I have ever heard. It was so distracting that the nurse asked if she should go help him. "No," I screamed, "I am having a baby here. He is just throwing up!" It was quite the scene.

In all of the pictures and video of Jake's birth, Brad is a little pale. I think he will forever be scarred by that experience. After all that, I did deliver our baby, and we brought home a sweet, but loud, baby boy, Jacob "Jake" Gunner Ewing.

Life was moving at a quick pace, and we were enjoying our happy family. We quickly found a great group of friends and began a class for young couples. We poured our lives into that class and the young couples that attended.

Brad was feeling led to lead worship, so he would experiment with his new found love of leading worship for our class. It was rough going at first, but they loved us anyway. I am learning increasingly that people love us more when we reveal our faults rather than when we pretend to be perfect. It was like we were all growing and learning together, this young class. We stayed up all hours the of night playing games, laughing, and eating tons of junk food.

There were several couples that really bonded. We laughed, we cried, we cooked, we cleaned; we did it all together. There was one couple, Patrick and Krystal Burns, who didn't yet have kids; they practically moved in with us. We spent nights cooking meals together. We played games all through the night.

One morning, Patrick and Krystal had spent the night and were asleep on our pull out couch in the living room. Drew had woken up especially early and slipped past our room to find Patrick and Krystal.

He was so excited that they were asleep in our living room that he crawled up on the bed and jumped as hard as his little legs would allow and landed right on top of Patrick. Patrick, immediately awoken from a dead sleep, was not too happy to be jumped on in a private place by a five year old. He handled it well considering the early morning injury.

They were a God send for us. They were surrogate parents to my kids. I was a young mom with young kids and needed all the help I could get. This couple loved my kids as if they were their own.

There will never be another couple like them that loved us and our kids that way. We didn't really know what we were doing, we just knew that God had brought us together and that we needed each other. Life was supremely good, and I was happier than I had ever been.

My favorite time of the night has always been when the kids are tucked into bed and I sink down into a hot bath, allowing the water to soak away the long day. Two young boys can wear a girl out. Life was sweet and exhausting.

Brad and I were living our secure and comfortable little life with few cares besides the every day. My life had finally settled into a happy routine: Marriage, family, church work, Bible studies. We had great friends who loved the Lord. As I leaned back in the bath and read from Beth Moore's "Things Pondered", it seemed to sink into my heart the same way my body was sinking into that warm water.

Yes, I long to walk by sight, but You're teaching eyes to see;
You know what You're doing, 'till then, I must believe.

I felt His great compassion, mercy unrestrained.
He let me mourn my losses and showed to me my gains.

I offered Him my future, and released to Him my past.
I traded in my dreams, for a plan He said would last.

I get no glimpse ahead; no certainties at all,
Except the presence of the One, who will not let me fall.

Are you also searching, for a life you planned yourself?
Have you looked in every corner?
Have you checked on every shelf?

Child, your ears have never heard, Your eyes have never seen,
Eternal plans He has for you are more than you could dream.

Perhaps you long to walk by sight, but He's teaching eyes to see;
He knows what He is doing, child, step out and believe.

I wanted to have that kind of faith. She nailed the kind of woman I wanted to be. I prayed that God would make me a woman that would step out and believe. When I was praying this, I sure wasn't thinking that my life was about to come crashing down. I wanted an easy faith; I wanted to live off the miracles God had already done.

I wanted him to take my mistakes and give me a platform to tell others about how good He is even when we make a horrible mess of our lives. I wanted THAT to be my story. It was a good story, don't you think?

I aspired to show young moms how to read and study their Bible. I was ready for God to take my life and use it. He did all of that. Just not the way that I expected. Not with the life that I had planned. It really never is, is it?

Are you also searching, for a life you planned yourself?
Have you looked in every corner? Have you checked on every shelf?

Child, your ears have never heard, your eyes have never seen,
Eternal plans He has for you are more than you could dream.

CHAPTER SEVEN
WHAT JUST HAPPENED?

A week later, we got up on a Sunday morning and went to church, as planned. It was one of those glorious Sundays, the sun was shining, and we had lunch with a huge group of our dearest friends right after church. It started out as the perfect day filled with faith, family, and friends.

We all sat and talked and laughed around a big table sharing meals for lunch. We talked of afternoon naps and Sunday night plans. After lunch, we drove home to take our typical Sunday naps. We got the boys out of the car, but Brad had me leave the car on because he had to run back to church to pick up something. He kissed me goodbye and said he would be home shortly. I hardly even gave him a second glance as he turned to go back to the car.

We should have just walked right in to our house but the week before I had been Holly Homemaker and changed our front door locks. Until that point, our front door didn't lock. We just walked in. I kept thinking about how dangerous that was, so I proudly changed the locks myself. There I stood, struggling to open my newly locked door when I realized that both boys were not with me. Brad had already gotten into the car to leave. The car engine whined into reverse as Jake, our youngest, ran for his daddy.

I heard a noise. I heard Brad screaming. Drew went running to see what had happened. Brad stood there holding Jake in his arms. Jake was moaning, "Daddy, Daddy, Daddy!" I ran in and called 911.

I could barely tell them my own address. Neighbors came out. Chaos erupted. We waited for the paramedics, and when they arrived, Brad got in the ambulance with Jake, who was still crying for his daddy. I just watched the ambulance drive away. I was standing there in the driveway, helpless. It all happened so fast.

My parents arrived and my dad took Drew home with him. My mom and I drove to the hospital in a frustrated and confused rush. We didn't even know how to get to the main hospital. I remember calling information and telling them that my son was just hit by a car and that I could not find the hospital. After a while, we finally found it.

We were scared to death. Down a long, bright, white hallway, too far from where Jake was, we sat in faded, worn out chairs. The room was too small for the number of chairs, but my family sat down and shut the door, the neutral walls closing us into the tiny space. The lights were dim, a sharp contrast to the blinding light just outside the door. A small lamp lit the corner, and we waited in silence. The only noise was the incessant tick tock of the large, schoolroom clock.

    We sat in hard chairs that made your back ache. There was no television, and no one said a word. Occasionally we would catch each other's eye, and silent fear filled the room. I wondered where Jake was and why I hadn't heard anything. The longer we sat, knee to knee to each other, the more I wondered how badly Jake was hurt. I begin replaying the accident in my head and sorting through what ending I could accept.

    Then a knock came at the door. The doctors pushed into the small room, wearing blue surgical scrubs, with a mask hanging down around their necks. I noticed the main doctor's voice shook as he said, "I am sorry, but we did everything we could and Jake did not make it." I can't even tell you what he died from. I am sure they told us, but the words made no sense to me. I didn't hear any of their explanations, any of their condolences. I couldn't understand what they were saying past the four small words that changed our life forever. Your son is dead.

My face got hot, blood thundered through my veins, my heart skipped a beat, and all the color left me. My little sister, Breanne, says she will never forget that look on my face. For a brief second, I thought I was going to be sick, right there in that waiting room, sick. I didn't know what to do. I don't think I felt anything. An invisible shell of merciful nothing enveloped me, guarding me from reality.

I could not believe it. I was trying to process through the rubble in my mind of what was going on. Sure, I knew he was hurt, very badly, but death? Never in a million years did I see that coming.

We thanked them and then got up and walked out of the room. I opened the door and walked back into the same bright, white hallway forever changed. Church members were scattered along the walls, nurses walking past with their stark white shoes squeaking down the hall and I turned to my left and saw some of our dearest friends in the world walking right up to us. Meggan wrapped her arms around me and asked me how Jake was? My head was right in the small of her neck right by her ear, tears scalded my eyes, and I whispered the two words that changed my life forever. "Jake's dead."

Suddenly I couldn't stand. My body could no longer hold itself up. In the recesses of my mind, I heard Meggan scream, "I'm losing her," and I felt like I was doing a free fall into a dark, deep hole. Then my world went dark.

Minutes later with a nurse leaning over me, I was lying on a hospital bed. The same room that they had just tried to help my little boy and now they were helping me. There was a stainless steel operating table covered in surgical green fabric. A huge light hung over the bed, revealing the fact that Jake was no longer being attended to.

I glanced over, and my mom was peering out at me with a terrified look on her face. I lay on that hospital bed looking out, trying to swallow, but my mouth felt full of cotton. The nurse handed me orange juice in a brown cup with a straw sticking out. I tried to drink the liquid and force myself to swallow the news of the death of my child.

My heart, my body, and my head didn't know how to process it all. I shut down and not for the last time. I just sat there staring at the wall. I looked up from the hospital bed and saw Brad and his close friend Josh walking down the hall, their dress shoes clanking against the white tile floor as they followed the policeman.

Their Sunday clothes were untucked and rumpled. Brad had taken off his dress shirt and removed the evidence of the accident with Jake. He stood there in a white undershirt looking like a scared kid.

He had to go to the police station and make a statement, and for the first time I saw him completely terrified of what the future held. Josh was following him and watching over him like a brother. I was concerned for him and scared for us. Yet, I just sat there, unable to move.

They asked me if I wanted to see Jake. I did. There he was lying on a metal table with a white blanket over him, just his head was sticking out. I reached up and touched a piece of his light brown hair that was hanging down near his eye. Understanding eluded me. How could this be happening?

They moved me to another hospital bed and pushed me into another room. As I lay there, our friends and family began pouring in. It was the strangest thing; I sat on this bed in the middle of the room, and people just stood against the peeling, papered walls of blue and beige, looking at me.

I could hear the quiet ticking of the clock above their heads but they all just stood there, staring past each other. The room was dark with little light peeking in from the lit hallways. No one knew what to do. The silence was deafening, each person unwilling to move, scared to speak. What is there to say?

Clinging close to the end of the bed, Meggan and my mom offered me water every few minutes. The other guests stood there looking at me. I could hear a few whispers every once, and a while but it was otherwise silent. I sat there on the bed in a trance-like state staring at the people closest to me like they were in a line up.

Eventually, someone broke the silence and said something. I'm sure someone prayed. Plans began to be made, and soon I got up from the bed and walked on unsteady legs out the back door of the hospital to a loading dock where a car was waiting for me. I didn't want to go back to our house, and everyone had decided it was best for us to go to my parents' house instead. I went along on autopilot just doing what I was told.

I overheard bits and pieces of conversations swirling around me that my parent's house would be best so that the news media couldn't get to us. Media? I thought that was very odd. Why would the news media want to talk to us? It dawned on me gradually, my son was dead and that was news.

I worried about Brad, but I didn't know how to get in touch with him. Later I found out that after the police questioned him, they had let him go. They had escaped any media attention and were en route to my parent's house, too.

Word was spreading, and arrangements were made to fly family into town. People came and went, dropping off food and extending their love. I remember someone told me that they would be praying for our marriage because 99% of people that have a child die get a divorce. "Thanks for that bit of encouragement, I will add that to my list of concerns," I thought. I knew they meant well, but maybe not the best time for that kind of advice.

I was given a prescription to calm me. I didn't think I was hysterical, but the doctor said it would take the edge off. Let me go ahead and tell you that there is no pill strong enough to take the edge off what had just happened, but I appreciated the medicine nonetheless.

Brad's parents arrived very soon after the accident; her boss had allowed them to use his private plane. Brad's mom said I opened the door for them smiling and hugging them, as if nothing had happened.

Pill or no pill, the truth is I didn't know how to act. Was I supposed to get on the floor and throw a fit, scream, cry my eyes out? I didn't know, so I just said hello, smiled, and hugged everyone that walked through the doors. Then I'd go sit on my mom's big purple couch, drinking gallons of coffee and hearing the hum of quiet whispers, shuffling feet, and the clatter of dishes being arranged in the kitchen.

My parents had a big basement, and Drew's friends came to help keep him entertained. They played and played in that basement. I was told later that Drew punched his best friend that night. I guess Drew didn't really know how to act either. I bet punching someone felt better and was healthier than stuffing emotions and smiling at guests the way I did.

Brad and his buddies took over the back porch. People were gathered in spots all over the house. I would walk past and see him out there writing something. Our eyes would meet occasionally, and we would just stare at the other, not sure what to say or do.

We hardly talked but knew the other was close by if we needed each other. A group of his buddies was sitting out there, and one was smoking cigarettes. I laughed to myself. My dad had just resigned as pastor of a large church in town, and I wondered what those "church people" would say about the young guy on the back porch smoking. I must admit that it gave me great amusement. Part of me wanted to sit out there and smoke with him. Give them just one more thing to talk about. I didn't. I was playing nice.

Brad is a song writer, and he processes life through music and lyrics. He was out there doing the only thing He knew to do, write. He sat out on the paved rock patio surrounded by people, a little piece of paper and pen balanced on his knee while smoke wafted around him, but he was in his own world writing these words:

The Lord giveth, and the Lord taketh away
Those words are hard to swallow, On a day like today
And though it's hard to understand, things go the way they do
Our God's alive and in our hearts, and He will see us through

They say when times are hard, it's a testing of our faith,

But surely we could've done without, the thing that happened today
We say that now and in our hurt, we feel it to be true
But later on and down the road, we'll see what God can do

A son is gone, a brother lost, this thing we cannot change
But by the Lord's Almighty hand, there's comfort to be claimed
He turns mistakes to miracles, we see it in many ways,
But never has it pierced our hearts, until this loss today.

And so we pray with all our heart, that Jake not go in vain,
But while he's in our Savior's lap, our God would get more praise
So Lord, our Jake is with You now, please tell him this for us,
That Momma, Daddy, and brother Drew,
are gonna stay here and trust

And that one sweet day we'll meet again outside those pearly gates,
You'll waddle down those golden streets,
And we'll join you .... Singin' praise! [7]

---

[7] A Family's Promise by Brad Ewing

CHAPTER EIGHT
THE RISING FOG

We decided to bury Jake in Brad's hometown of Bossier City, LA. It seemed like the best place - Brad's family would always live there. We picked the casket, the casket cover, speakers, the music, the church. Decision after decision.

I felt like an outsider looking in, watching myself. It was as if I was moving and doing what I needed to get things done, but it wasn't really me. I was on autopilot. No one prepares you for these kind of situations. No one tells you how to grieve days after the accident. My uncle says, God gives us "trouble grace," the grace we need for the trouble we are in. God shields you from feeling everything at once; it's a merciful limbo.

A kind doctor had given us sleeping pills to help get us through the nights. My mom, who never takes much medicine, decided she needed to take a sleeping pill to finally get some rest.

I remember her standing in her closet, and as the pill began to take effect, she went delusional. It was hilarious. She was trying to put on her pajamas and couldn't stand to get her feet in them. She was kind of rolling around trying to get her pajama pants on.

Finally, she got in bed, looked at my dad, and told him he had two noses. It was priceless. Not only did God give us the grace we needed but some much needed comic relief as well. We had some rough days ahead of us.

I think the visitation was the worst. The family came early to have our own time with Jake. Our very last time to be with him on earth. I walked into the room, and there he was, my Jake, lying there, stiff and cold.

It was mid-afternoon, and Jake should have been waking up from a nap and ready to play. He should have been standing up in his bed yelling for me to get him out instead of lying flat in the casket. His hands should have been raised up waiting on me to get him out. I used to pick him up from the crib and listen to him squeal in delight as he ran down our hallway towards the kitchen for a snack.

I picked him up, but I couldn't set him down to run around. I saw his face, but there was no light behind his eyes. Yesterday his eyes glowed with excitement; his face was lit with joy and wonder.

I held him, but it wasn't *really* him. My Jake, the Jake that walked a step behind us because he couldn't keep up and would yell "I comin, I comin" in the sweetest toddler voice you have ever heard, was gone.

His favorite camouflage blanket, a blanket that followed him everywhere, a blanket that was just as much apart of him as his hand, was lying on him, but he wasn't holding it in his chubby fingers. The blanket was as lifeless as he was. I rocked him for a while, his body stiff and straight, not bending to my touch the way he used to. My own heart feeling chilled and lifeless, too.

The searing reality of seeing his body in a casket was heart wrenching. It was a small wooden box dressed up in white shiny fabric; but it was still a casket, and my two year old was lying in it just as if it was a crib.

It held a lifeless body, and the sight singed a scar on my heart forever. That picture awakened a new reality for me. Until heaven, Jake would never again reach up and hold my hand. He would never again ask for his momma. I would never hear him say 'I comin' again. His smile would never light up another room. His life was over, and it seemed mine was too.

Then the ordeal continued; people began to arrive, and we were still up front by the casket. We got caught up in a line of people who for hours and hours wanted to talk to us and show their love and support.

I appreciated most of them, I really did. It was just so hard to stand there. At one point, Brad's Uncle Chris, stood behind me and literally held me up. My oldest sister Angela's husband arrived with the most thoughtful gift, my own chap-stick. It is a common family joke that Jon always has chap-stick and is a germiphobe, so we like to borrow his chap-stick and watch him squirm. It was just what I needed at that moment to get me a few more minutes through that line.

I took a brief break in the line and walked outside. I walked into the foyer of the funeral home, and one of my dad's good friends from Dallas, Tim Horner, was sitting in a brown leather chair in the front of the funeral home. He looked at me with these piercing, concerned blue eyes, and I don't even know if we said a word to each other. His look of love and sympathy was enough. We just sat there for a few seconds, both stunned. I think it was one of the sweetest things someone could have done. No words were needed that day, just the troubled expression and silence. I went back to my duties in the receiving line slightly stronger.

The line continued and only seemed to increase as the night wore on. My parents were to the left of me; and I watched as they gracefully received and accepted people who had not been very nice in their days of ministry, and I remember boiling inside.

Had I not had God's "trouble grace," I would have acted just like Drew and punched someone that night. So, I smiled and hugged and accepted their condolences, pretending that what they had done to my parents didn't affect me then. In hindsight, I kind of wish I had punched someone. That would have been the only time I could have gotten away with something like that. (Smile)

In those dark moments, my friends' thoughtfulness amazed me. Just as Moses had friends that held his arms up when he couldn't do it on his own, Brad and I had people that stood in the gap for us. The amount of work and effort that went into holding us together was tremendous.

Josh made hundreds of trips to the airport and thousands of phone calls. Meggan, my best friend, kept the house organized and running. She answered phones, wrote down who came with food, accepted a million flowers, and cleaned the kitchen over and over again. She probably made more coffee that week than she has in her entire life. She was our rock; she took care of everything and everyone.

There was Lindsay who loved on me in her quiet and caring way. She showered me with Scripture, prayer, and hugs. Christy and Autumn showed up and dressed Brad and Drew for all the events.

Krystal and Patrick, who had moved to Amarillo a few months previously, no longer upset that Drew had come close to ruining his chance at having children, stepped right back into their roles as nanny of Drew. It was as if they had never left. It brought instant relief to see them by his side. It was so normal, the way things were - the way things were supposed to be.

I went to my cousin Christy's house, and she allowed me to borrow the most beautiful silver and black silk dress. It was perfect, just what I needed. I needed her style to get me through the funeral day because every southern girl knows that when we are falling apart on the inside, we dress up the outside. (wink)

I remember the way our young couple's class showed their love and support. Couples we had poured our lives into were now pouring back. As dark as the days were, we did see beautiful pictures of the church acting as the body it was created to be.

CHAPTER NINE
GAINING SOME PERSPECTIVE

The funeral was a blur. Drew made it through about twenty minutes, and then his five year old attention span kicked in. Our children's minister took him out and let him play dart guns. I sometimes think I should have gone with them.

Instead, I sat, occasionally drying my eyes as tears rolled down. I thought about my oldest sister; she was 37 weeks pregnant and couldn't travel, so they played the funeral for her over the phone. I wondered what that was like for her. Not really getting to say goodbye to Jake, just listening in.

My uncle preached the funeral. How he made it through that day, I will never know. He said something though that brought me such comfort. He said, "Jake was running to his earthly father's arms and was met by his Heavenly Father's arms." It brought instant comfort and relief for me. I really understood it there for the first time that Jake did get the better end of the deal. He met his heavenly Father who was waiting for him with arms open wide.

While my heart ached that I would never hold Jake here on this earth, I was extremely comforted that this was not the end. The funeral gave me hope knowing that one day I would see

Jake again. I walked out of the funeral service knowing that because of Jesus, I had a way to see Jake again. While my heart hurt that I would not hear the words, "I comin" from Jake, I was reassured that Jake would one day here the words "I am coming" from me. We grieve, yes, but with hope.

Quite a few people were saved that day. Brad's biological dad was saved, and everyone was excited about their redeemed lives. I was mad. My sister, Angela said it best, "We wanted them to get their lives together on their own time." Angela is great at adding comic relief to the bleakest of times.

You should have heard her response when I told her about the prayer I prayed in the bathtub. She looked me dead in the face and said, "You could have given us a little warning after praying a prayer like that!" She said what we were all thinking. Why did our family have to suffer so that others could come to know Jesus?

The more people marveled about how many people were saved and how many lives were changed, the more I hurt. I felt like I was trying to balance the bad that had happened against the good that could come out of it. The scales were never even in my mind.

It didn't matter to me what good had come from this event, I still lost. It felt like I had lost everything. It felt like my son was a sacrificial lamb, led to the slaughter for the sake of someone else.

Not long after funeral, I was going through Beth Moore's Jesus, The One and Only Bible study. She says that Jesus is the only sacrificial lamb and God **did** lead him to the slaughter for me and for every one of us. I would not have done it. Given the choice, I would have let my son live. God didn't. The pain of losing a son is beyond description, and that fact that God choose his only Son, Jesus to give up his life for us, stuns me. There are not enough words to utter my appreciation for that kind of sacrifice.

In order to keep myself from burning in anger towards others every time they commented on how much good had come from Jake's death, I had to come to a very important crossroad of belief in my life. I had to know that God does not cause bad or evil. God did not choose for my son to die, but He did allow it.

God brought good out of our bad - He didn't cause the bad in order to make the good, though. That was a huge truth for me. Just like Genesis 50:20 "As for you, you meant evil against me, but God meant it for good, to bring it about that many people should be kept alive, as they are today." God takes the evil and brings forth good, not the other way around.

God didn't create Jake to be a sacrificial lamb - He used Jake's short life to show others how good He is. I had to make small, calculated choices each day about my view of God. Was I going to blame God and be bitter or allow God to work? It is the small decisions that I think we don't really even know we are making that bring us either to a healthy view of tragedy or a distorted view that makes us bitter in the end.

Each day I was having to take up my cross and follow Him. What that meant in the midst of days like these was trusting that God was good. When your son has only been dead a few days, choosing to believe that God is good is extremely important, and I think it shaped how I eventually dealt with my grief.

When I was in sixth grade, I was forced by a kind youth worker to learn Jeremiah 29:11 "For I know the plans I have for you says the Lord, plans to prosper you and not to harm you, plans for a hope and future." Thank you, Mrs. Kunkle, because that verse showed me that God's plans for me was for my good and not to harm me.

Even though at the moment they felt harmful, God really did have plans for my hope and future. I had to choose daily, minute by minute, to trust in that verse and that God's Word was really true.

Michael Catt in his book, The Power of Desperation says "Brokenness is not something we sign up for. It's not the elective we choose in order to get an easy grade. But it is a necessity if we are going to be useful to the Master.[8]" This was not how I had planned my life to turn out. I wanted to walk by faith and not by sight, but I wanted it the easy way.

---

[8] Michael Catt, "The Power of Desperation."

CHAPTER TEN
A TIME FOR EVERYTHING

It was like the funeral that never ended. Since we had decided to bury Jake in Brad's hometown, we had to all fly there and have the burial in another state; which meant another set of people and another group to face. I was exhausted, and there wasn't an end in sight.

We all booked our flights and prepared for another week of saying goodbye. I honestly don't remember flying to Bossier. I can't even tell you how we got to the airport. I am sure Josh took us. He took everyone to the airport.

I don't remember getting there or what we did that day. I guess the medicine the doctors gave me was better than I thought since I can't remember much. (smile)

I do remember that my sister was close to having her baby in the midst of all of this and we were unsure of how to plan for a unexpected burial AND new baby. We had planned for the burial on September 9, 1999. Jake's birthday. Just two short years with Jake here on this earth. It just felt right to celebrate his earthly birthday with his heavenly one.

Early that morning, my sister had a baby boy and by mid- afternoon we had buried Jake. My mom looked at me and quoted Ecclesiastes 3:1-2 "There is a time for everything, and a season for every activity under the heavens: a time to be born and a time to die."

This is coming from a mom who left one daughter right after the delivery of a precious baby boy to sit with her other daughter as she buried hers. She had to rest in the peace that God had appointed each event and only He could walk us through this valley of the shadow of death.

My mom was showing me how to handle Jake's death in small and easy to handle chunks. A whispered verse, a hug, or new sunglasses showed me that I just needed to trust His appointed timing for everything. It wasn't smothering attention or a distant mother; somehow she found the perfect balance of what I needed.

On another bright Sunday afternoon, I sat under a covered tent with chairs lined up in front of the littlest casket I had ever seen, wondering what had happened to the life I had planned. Whose life was this? How does one live a life after this? I cried at the right times; I bowed my head at the right times; I stood and followed the others past the casket, dropping my flower on top of Jake, wishing I could just crawl in there with him.

I was scared. The events were wrapping up. I was no longer going to be on display; my life was about to return back to semi-normal. Could I make it? Would our family survive? Would our marriage survive? Questions and doubts rolled around in my head as I watched flower after flower drop on the casket. As each flower dropped, a new doubt or concern rose up inside of me. I no longer asked why, but how? How were we going to make it through this?

Then it was time for the ultimate birthday party. The day we buried Jake was exactly two years from the day Brad went crawling to the bathroom floor while I was in labor. It was exactly two years from the day that we held our loud and lively Jake in our arms for the first time, and that day was now the celebration of his birth into a body that only Christ can provide.

A group of ladies that I hardly even knew spent hours preparing hundreds of balloons. Each of us was given a colored balloon, and we all let them go up into the air, "up to Jake." The sight of hundreds of balloons rising about the trees to the sky will forever be imprinted in my memory. I will formally apologize to any pilot who might have been flying a plane that day. I am very sorry for the havoc that must have caused. We plead total insanity.

The sight of balloons can still cause my heart to skip a few beats. Memories flood back to that day every time I see one. Each year on Jake's birthday, we release balloons in memory of him. A celebration of eternal life. A life that Jake now has that will never taste death. We long for the day when we can enjoy it with him.

Two days after we buried Jake, 9/11 shook our country. We were awakened in Dallas to a second nightmare. My world had already crumbled, and it looked like the rest of the world was joining me.

The whole country was feeling just like me, in a state of shock and astonishment that death had so personally touched our lives. Slowly the reality of what had happened seeped into my overwhelmed heart, and I just wanted Jesus to come back. I just wanted all of it to be over.

It took days to make it home because of 9/11. The airlines had shut down; the world was reeling from the attack. We were numb. Brad and Josh wound up driving back home. I think Brad needed a few days alone with his buddy to adjust to our new world. Drew and I flew home a few days later once the airlines opened up.

I remember sitting there waiting in the airport with Drew playing just like any five year old. It was very quiet in the airport. Everyone was scared. Drew suddenly made a loud shooting noise, and I thought we were going to get tackled by security. Everyone realized it was just a boy playing, and nervous laughter erupted. It kind of broke the ice for all of us.

Drew is what kept me going those days after. I still had to be a mom, and that kept me moving moment by moment. I just wanted to go to sleep and not wake up, but I had a boy who needed to be fed, needed to go to school, and needed to do the every day things a boy does. We continued to live with my parents, so I did have some much needed help.

The nights were the worst. Drew would cry out for his brother for almost an hour every night. We all sat around his bed trying to comfort him. He would just yell, "I want my Jake. I want my Jake."

We were lost on how to help him. We sat with him, lay with him, tried to soothe him. We were hurting so bad too that there was not much left for us to offer him. We were just there, all existing under the same roof trying to get through one more night.

Drew would eventually tire himself out and drift off to sleep. He went to see a play therapist, and that seemed to help him some. She would play with him and walk through many of his emotions with him.

One thing she used was sand. Sand is supposedly a healing agent for kids. They would rake sand with cars and other toys in it. He seemed to like to do it. We had a special friend who made us sand containers so that we could play with the sand at home. Maybe that is why I like the beach so much; the sand is therapeutic to my soul.

CHAPTER ELEVEN
LETTERS OF HOPE

We had an outpouring of cards and letters, and each one was very special. I read story after story speaking of God's faithfulness in times of loss from people I barely knew. I still have boxes of cards. People's affection for me during that time was humbling.

Papa Johns is my favorite pizza, and the owner of Papa Johns actually called and said he was having any kind of pizza we wanted delivered. I love pizza, and this spoke volumes to me - I savored each piece and poured extra garlic sauce on each one. The thoughtfulness of total strangers was a part of the healing for me.

One letter stood out to me more than the rest. It was from Ginger, my mentor from college. My hands trembled as I opened the letter. Three pages, typed! I longed for her wisdom, her knowledge. She had lived through our nightmare; her son had also died when she was younger. She would know what I needed to hear. I grabbed a cup of coffee, unfolded the pages, and sat on the purple couch. Tears immediately filled my eyes, her words jumped off the page and into my heart.

Dear Kasey,

Kasey I want you to know that I am here and that even though I don't know what it is like to lose your precious Jake, I do know what it was like to lose Matt.

I do know some things that you will have to face now. Now that the friends and family are not with you every minute, now that Brad has to go back to work, now that you are both wounded and need the other more than you ever have and they are hurting with the same intensity that you are.

I do know that you both will heal in different ways and at different speeds. What may comfort you, may drive Brad insane and vice versa. Don't expect it to be the same for both of you. And don't think the other one is insensitive because of it.

My biggest advice is give yourself time. For many reasons, you are hurt and in shock like most people on this earth will happily never know.

Two, you need to let the LORD minister to you in a way that NO HUMAN BEING can. LEAN ON HIM .... hard. Tell HIM everything you are feeling and let HIM do what only HE can.

Heaven becomes a reality. Eternity becomes a reality, once death becomes a reality. Oh, Kasey I wish I had magic words or formulas, but I don't.

I just give you JESUS ...... and HE is enough.

I love you,
Ginger.

  I needed those words from Ginger, I needed a face who had survived the death of a child. I believed whatever she said because she had been down the dark road I was traveling.

Another letter that I treasured was from Beth Moore. I had sent her a letter briefly explaining how I had read her poem just one week before Jake's death.

I told her how I appreciated her and her ministry. I grew up spiritually on Beth Moore. I used to joke that my kids would recognize her voice over mine!

What shocked the pants off me was a letter in return. I could not believe it. She was a spiritual giant in my eyes and I had in my hands a hand written letter. I just kept reading it over and over. (FYI, she still likes to use lots of exclamation points.) She wrote...

My Dear, Dear Kasey,

I want you to know, Precious little sister, that I have bawled for you just as you have for me. There is NO comparison in the depth of loss. Dear one, but I am at least so thankful God could have used some little something I wrote. Your loss is so great, surely none greater and even now I cry - but not only for sadness. Oh, Kasey, I also cry for joy. Satan will not win here, will he? He would have been too sure he could destroy both you and your husband through this. BUT HE WILL NOT WIN.

I am so thankful, dear one, that in your unfathomable grief, you are refusing to give up your faith. I will never throw away the letter you sent. The words will ring my heart forever: "I know now more than I ever could have that EVERYTHING I have ever known and read about our God is TRUE and can't be changed." Child, that statement rocked the gates of hell and released the hosanna of 10,000 angles. Grieve - Yes - how could you not?! But not as those who have no hope!" (1 Thes. 4).

Psalm 126 that says "the one who chooses to sow the seed (that's the Word of God according to the parable of the sower) with tears will come out with SONGS of joy and waving sheaves."

I am also reminded of Isaiah 25:6-9. Read it carefully. You will be able to say as you see Him face to face "Surely this is our God and I trusted Him[9]." He is worthy of your trust! He can take every outpouring of your heart. He will raise you both mighty warriors of the faith and Jake's life will speak life and breath."

I will be praying for you and thinking of you so often. I am so proud of you, Kasey. You are NOT missing the grace of God and letting a bitter root grow that defiles many. (Heb. 12:15) You are doing the hard thing but the right thing. GOD WILL BRING FORTH A HARVEST and you will have all eternity with your precious Jake. In the meantime life will seem long, but when you get there and Jesus is holding him and waiting to hand him to you, it will seem the blink of an eye.

Stay faithful, precious little sister! An eternal work of glory is under way - one with huge and wonderful repercussions.

I love you,
Beth Moore

One practice I began after getting this letter was to put the promise of Psalms 126 to the test. I got a pack of spiral notecards and wrote out Scriptures that I needed to cling to for the moments of darkness that would inevitably set in. When my friends are walking through a hurtful time, I give them a cheap spiral of notecards. On each notecard is a Scripture that speaks life and breath to a dark and dying soul.

---

[9] Isaiah 25:9

Here are a few examples for you to fully grasp what sowing the Word means. I would write out Isaiah 26:3-4 "You will keep in perfect peace, those whose minds are steadfast, because they trust in you. Trust in the LORD forever, for the LORD, the LORD himself, is the Rock eternal."

I would read this and say back to God. "Lord, keep me in perfect peace. Give me a steadfast mind that fully trusts in you. You are my eternal rock, my LORD, let me trust in you no matter what." Then I would turn over to the next verse. Isaiah 43: 1-3 "But now, this is what the LORD says— he who created you, Jacob, he who formed you, Israel: Do not fear, for I have redeemed you; I have summoned you by name;you are mine. When you pass through the waters, I will be with you; and when you pass through the rivers, they will not sweep over you. When you walk through the fire, you will not be burned; the flames will not set you ablaze." I say back to Him, "You created me; you formed me. I do fear the future; help me to not fear what is ahead. You tell me that I am yours, so I give this back to You. I can't do this. You must move here. You promise me that when I pass through the waters, I will not be swept away. Your word says that when I walk through the fire, I will not be burned. Do your work here, Lord. Do what only you can do."

I do this same thing for notecard after notecard. Scripture is our weapon against the enemy. I had to learn how to use it, or I was going to sink, fast.

I must be honest here and say that this is hard work. Grief is a fight. The words that I received from friends like Ginger and Beth Moore encouraged me to keep fighting. They were hopeful words that spoke a charge over me to be faithful and not give up, words that forecasted I could and would walk humbly with God through this time and He would reap a harvest from it.

Their trust in me, that I would prevail through this trial, gave me the greatest gift, hope. Hope that through this, God would reign and the powers of hell would not stand against our family. I cannot tell you how important it is to have those around you that speak truth into you life. This is not a time to surround yourself with people who only tell you what you want to hear. We must have people built into our lives who will speak words of prophetic hope into our lives.

Even though I cherished these letters, the battle was raging. I felt as if people were being kind only because of the situation we were in. Our family circumstances, coupled with some crazy church politics, had me all in a tizzy. I was an emotional time bomb ready to explode.

There was so much to deal with emotionally that I couldn't think straight, and I was just plain mad. I can admit and realize now that I probably used this situation as a safe way to let my quietly growing rage slip out here and there. It was a righteous anger in my mind, and the church "politicians" became an easy target for me to unleash my venom. Recognizing this, I finally sent Ginger another email. I still have her response to my complaints.

Kasey,

I know you are hurting and angry and worried and frustrated. But Kasey now is not the time to forget all that the LORD has taught you two about HIS sovereignty. He can handle whatever is in your path and HE will equip you to be able to handle it.

I love you, stop flaying away at the air and start TRUSTING ...... this is a TEST, don't fail it.

So this is what I (we) have discovered over these last few years, the only thing that matters in life is obedience, especially in the hard days of your life, the trials, the testing, the tribulation or even in the joyous and sweet days.

Ginger

Ginger sent me two devotionals, each one asking me if I was ready to be poured out as an offering. Was I willing to sacrifice my ideas of how my life was supposed to turn out and allow God to do His work? Was I willing to follow Him when it hurt and it wasn't pretty, when I was treated wrongly, when I was dismissed, when I was wrongly accused? Would I follow then? Ginger was showing me that I had to get my emotions under control.

I had to choose to serve God when it was a sacrifice - when it wasn't easy, when I didn't feel like it. These devotions were instrumental in changing my thinking. In the depths of our hearts, I think we come to Jesus for what He can do for us. In my heart of hearts, I really thought that I didn't deserve all that was happening to me.

My life seemed unfair. Why were my friends having babies, and I had buried mine? Why did my husband not have a secure job when he was working for a church? Why did this all happen to me? I was a good person; I was seeking after the Lord, I was teaching Bible studies. I was discipling other ladies.

I felt as if I was finally doing it all right for the first time in my life and I was somehow being punished. I am thankful for

Ginger who gently reminded me that because of Jesus, we don't get what we deserve. We don't have to suffer through what we deserve because He exchanged His life for our punishment. Now He is asking me to do the same.

    Was I willing? Yes!

    Was it hard? Yes!

    Was it painful? Yes!

    Would I make the same choice all over again? Yes!

    I stand in awe of how God orchestrated events so that Ginger would be the lady that discipled me years before, a lady of wisdom and heartache so similar to mine. Ginger was living out the call God places on each one of us, allowing God to speak to her, and then sharing with others.

    When I emailed Ginger and asked her for permission to use the words she had spoken to me, I got this response. "Of course you can use anything in the book that will minister to someone else. Any words I wrote to you were those the LORD comforted me with. I am so proud of you and know that the LORD will bring glory to HIMSELF now and at the revelation of JESUS CHRIST through your words of encouragement to others."

Every one needs a Ginger in their lives.

There is a verse in Matthew 10:27 "What I tell you in the dark, speak in the daylight; what is whispered in your ear, proclaim from the roofs."

Ginger was allowing God to use her to reveal His truths to me. What Ginger had learned in her darkest hours, she was speaking right into my own darkness. I think we resist having people like this in our lives. We pick friends, churches, and pastors who make us feel good.

Ginger was good for me in many ways, but mostly because in her kind and gentle manner, she told me what I needed to hear. There is a temptation to remove people from our lives who don't agree with us or who hold us to a higher standard.

Flee that temptation - find a church, small group and friends who will call your bluff. Looking back, I can see how written words from faithful people shaped the woman I am becoming. I desired, and still do, for their words to become true in my life.

CHAPTER TWELVE
IT IS WELL

Brad and I just kind of existed together. We were muddling through unknown waters. We woke up one day and found ourselves in the deep end and we were just flailing around trying not to drown. We were just trying to get through one day at a time.

He is a night owl and spent most of his days in a haze playing his guitar and writing music through the night. There were times, in the deep of the night, he would slip into the bed. I could feel him next to me, and he would scoot in close and just hold me. Tears would roll down both of our faces, sometimes quiet, soft tears. Sometimes we huddled together sobbing loudly. Not many words were spoken, but tears of heartache bonded us together when words couldn't.

He went back to work shortly after the accident. I think he just needed something to do. Work was not a good place for Brad though. A new pastor had been hired, and Brad was the son-in-law of the old pastor. It was a very hard situation. We knew that they wanted us to leave; we even got word that Brad was going to be fired, but we were a political nightmare. How does a church fire an employee that just lost his son? They couldn't. It wouldn't look good. So he stayed on.

One night, Brad was taking a walk and felt like he couldn't breathe. He sat down on the sidewalk, crying out to God "I can't do this anymore. Please, let me quit." His world was too much to handle.

Looking back, we should have made him take more time off. After much discussion, he and I felt it was best for Brad to resign and do just that, take some time off. In a considerable kindness, the church gave him a great severance which would allow for a much needed break.

I have heard of many people who quickly go back to work and re-enter their old world, only to find they can't handle the day to day. I think we were so disrupted by the loss that we longed for a sense of normalcy so we jumped back into the day to day before we were ready.

Not long after Brad's resignation, we headed to Louisiana to stay with Brad's parents for a while. We thought it might help us heal and rest. We were able to go to church as non-staff and begin our life-long healing process.

I thought Brad's hometown would be best for Brad, but he seemed to slip further and further away from us. He slept more during the day and played his guitar most of the night. We began to function on a different schedule, just passing each other every now and then. I was unsure what to do. I felt like I was losing him.

We were both hurting so badly and didn't know how to come together to help each other. Bewildered, we often just looked at each other. We didn't blame each other; we didn't fight; we didn't hash out who should have done what; we didn't really even communicate. Silence.

We just lived near each other. We co-existed. There was wisdom in the silence. Not that we did it on purpose but we knew of places we shouldn't travel and baggage we didn't want to carry, so we stayed quiet. Scared to speak in fear of what we might say.

But I missed him. I missed his smile, his love of life. Brad makes me fun. On my own I am serious and uptight. Brad loosens me up. He brings joy to our house, and he had lost his joy and our whole family was feeling the effects. I missed so much of our old life, but I didn't know how to get it back.

We had such a good life, we had great friends, we were doing ministry together. We lost all of that, too, on top of Jake. There was so much loss at once.

Finally, one night I was in the bath, crying out to God to help us. We couldn't go on like this anymore. Brad walked in; I gently said, "Brad we lost Jake, and now it feels like we have lost you too. We need you." He looked shocked and a bit hurt. I was immediately hurt for him.

He didn't know what to do. He was heartbroken and shattered. He left the house and went to see my uncle. I don't know what was said, but Brad slowly began to pull out from his shell. He began to read a book by John Eldredge called Wild at Heart.

I will forever be grateful for that book. It awakened a dying passion in him to live, to live for God, to see joy in life again. It was just what he needed at that moment. Brad and I slowly began to talk again, to laugh occasionally, to hold hands, to hug more often. We began the tedious job of rebuilding our lives together, one small brick carefully laid on top of another.

Our counselor told us to be aware that men and women grieve differently, and she helped us understand each other's process. The counselor helped us so much and was instrumental in teaching us how to grieve together.

Drew continued to meet with the play therapist who helped him work through what he saw, how he felt, and how to respond. The main thing Drew's therapist told us as his sessions were coming to an end was that kids take their cues from their parents. If we make it, Drew will make it. If Drew sees healthy grief, he will grieve healthily. It's Parenting 101: model the behavior you want to see in your kids, and most likely they will follow.

I highly recommend Godly, Christian counseling. Counseling is not a taboo. It is a way to help us navigate through life. We must all drop our pride and admit when we need help. Help is a good thing!

Our counselor walked Brad and me through many land mines just waiting to erupt. One of the biggest things she taught us was that it is okay to feel two emotions at the same time. The same way that the Psalms are full of doubt and faith at the same time. Many of the Psalmists wrote out of a broken heart and a place of doubt, yet they never let go of hope and faith in God's character and promises.

A close childhood friend of mine watched her daddy die of cancer, and I watched her grieve many years after Jake's death. I suffered along with her in silence as she experienced a daughter's worst nightmare. She wrote one day that "It is well with my soul, but I am not alright[10]." This one quote resonated very deep inside me and describes how I felt that summer after Jake's death. I was not okay, but it was well with my soul. There was a deep underlying trust that God was going to get us through.

My friend's comments remind me of the the story of the Shunamite woman tucked away in Second Kings, Chapter 4 and 8. Do you remember the story?

This woman notices Elisha, and then builds on a room to her house for him to give him a place to eat, pray, and rest. Elisha offers to grant her a request in return for her kindness. She asks for nothing, but Elisha notices that she is barren and then declares that she will have a son within the next year.

Her response is, "No, my lord!... Please, man of God, don't mislead your servant!" My guess is that she has been wanting a child for so long but was tired of the disappointment

---

[10] Amy Lawson http://snoodlings.com/

of a barren womb. Her thought is that it would be easier to be disappointed with no children than to deal with the devastation of finally conceiving, only to lose the child.

The honest truth is that God doesn't want us to desire anything or anyone more than we desire Him. The Lord gave the Shunammite woman this longing for a child, but He is going to take her through her worst fear in order for her to know that He can be trusted and deserves to be first in her life.

God allowed her to have a baby boy but then allowed him to become sick and die. She then brings the child to Elisha's room and leaves to go find Elisha. While looking for Elisha, she is asked by Elisha's servant if she is ok. Her reply is shocking. She says, "It is well." She had just lost a son moments before, and her response is "It is well"?! Her heart was set on finding Elisha, and she wasn't going to rest until she had met him face to face.

She wouldn't have to wait long. Laying hold of the prophet's feet, she says in verse 28, "Did I ask for a son? Did I not say, 'do not deceive me'?" The agony of her grief jumps off the pages of Scripture as she questions the prophet. Her son is dead, and she seems to want some answers as to why.

My words with Elisha might have gone something like this: *Elisha, this is exactly what I was trying to avoid! I did not want a child if it meant I was going to lose a child. The Lord gave me this child, and now I have lost him. So, what are you going to do about it?* Elisha seems deeply concerned and follows the woman back to her home. Eventually, the boy was given back his physical life. She had gotten her son back. However, when she started out in pursuit of Elisha, I don't think she knew how this whole thing was going to turn out. And that's why her faith is astonishing to me. She couldn't have known the ending, but she was going to the one she knew could help.

In the same way this woman went to the prophet Elisha for help, I can go to the only One that can truly handle my grief. And I think if we really understood the power of God, telling Him would be all we would need.

Not all of us get our hoped for ending to God's testing. I didn't. I didn't see God raise Jake from the dead, but I am seeing Him raise our hearts from the deepest, darkest place I have ever been.

No, I am not okay. I might never be, but it is well with my soul.

I often got the question in passing, "Hey, how are you?" and I never knew how to answer. Did they really want to know how I was? Honestly, I was dying inside. Did they want to know that? Did they really want to know that the question of "How are you?" offended me? Did they really want me to voice the dark parts of my soul? I didn't think so, but to simply lie wasn't an option either.

What the story of the Shunammite woman taught me is that I can tell others I am okay because I know Who to go to with my troubles. This woman taught me how to handle myself in times of uncertainty. She showed me it was acceptable to reveal my deepest grief to the One who could heal my hurt.

The Shunammite knew that Elisha was the one man who gave her her son and he was the only man she unleashed her grief upon. I don't want to tell you okay when I am not, and this story gave me permission to go to the One that can handle my grief.

There is a verse in Proverbs about not casting your pearls before swine. The verse doesn't necessarily teach that those around us are swine but we can learn from the principle. In my quest to be real and authentic, I became one who spilled every thought that crossed my mind. It wasn't pretty. There is a fine line between authentic and mean. I was closer mean. If I didn't agree with you, you would know it. I prided myself on my honesty. God showed me that I was honestly wrong.

First Corinthians 13, the love chapter, tells us that we can be a prophet, teacher, and all kinds of useful things but without love, we are nothing. Now, sometimes the most loving thing you can do for a person is be honest and truthful even if it hurts. This was not what I was doing; I was spewing venom in the name of being real.

We need to be like the Shunammite woman take our issues to the only ONE who can handle our issues and hurts. We can use this truth in all aspects of our lives.

Is your husband's boss a jerk? Well, tell on his boss to the Big Boss, and in front of others just simply say it is well. If your husband is not loving to you, don't go around telling the world how awful he is; tell God. If we really understand the power of God, telling Him is all we need. Once we tell him, we can honestly look others in the face and say it is well with our souls.

CHAPTER THIRTEEN
CHOOSING TO WORSHIP

The evening was the hardest time for me. When the sun goes down, darkness creeps up all around you. The protection of the daylight fades, and you are left with your thoughts. I would lie in bed and replay the accident over and over, changing the outcome if I had just done this or not done that.

My dad had an old CD called Christian relaxation where he walked a person through the process of Biblical mediation and I would do that over and over until I fell asleep. I would do anything to prevent those minutes of pure quiet and darkness. My mind settled in after a long day, and all I could do was think.

I never wanted to go to bed; I just wanted to be asleep. The quiet scared me. My thoughts were punishing me, and I didn't know how to get them to stop. No good can come from replaying and rehashing in my mind what had happened. I couldn't change what happened that day, so I had to learn to live with it.

Controlling my thoughts was the biggest battle I faced, one of the biggest battles we all face. It is imperative we learn this in our Christian walk. How do we change our thoughts? Scripture tells us in Romans 12:2 "Do not conform to the pattern of this world, but be transformed by the renewing of your mind. Then you will be able to test and approve what God's will is — his good, pleasing and perfect will."

Scripture is the only way to renew your mind. When my thoughts began to go in the wrong direction, blame myself, blame Brad, blame God, blame whoever was around - I had to stop those thoughts and say, "No! I refuse to think on this."

I had to choose to think about something else. I had to make myself concentrate on other things. It was a war. The battle was fierce and I often got bloodied up fighting it. Somedays I won and other days Satan had a party with me. I guess part of me thought that Satan might just give me a break, ease up on me a bit. I was wrong.

Satan is not a respecter of grief. In fact, that is when he goes for the jugular. 1 Peter 5:8 says "Be self-controlled and alert. Your enemy the devil prowls around like a roaring lion looking for someone to devour." He is ready to devour and if we are not careful in our times of deepest grief, we can leave the gates of our heart wide open.

So what do we do? How do we fight when we are wounded?

We worship.

Both Job and David did this as their response to the death of those they loved dearly. 2 Samuel 12: 20 says "Then David got up from the ground. After he had washed, put on lotions and changed his clothes, he went into the house of the LORD and worshiped." Job 1:20 says "At this, Job got up and tore his robe and shaved his head. Then he fell to the ground in worship." When faced with terrible circumstances, both of these men reacted in worship.

At this time in my life I didn't have the words to worship. I was completely empty. An album called "Psalms" by Shane and Shane became my worship. Each Psalm became my cry to God - I wore this album out. I started running right after the accident. There was something about putting headphones on and going out and pounding pavement that I needed.

It hurt and it felt good all at the same time. I would blare music in my ears and just run with sweat pouring down my face. When nothing else around me felt good, running gave me a small dose of relief. I loved it. I needed it. God used that to release the pent up tension, anger, and aggression. It was a practical way to vent my frustrations.

There were times I had Steven Curtis Chapman's Bring It On blasting in my ears and I would sing at the top of my lungs, daring Satan to touch us. Then I would run with tears streaming down my face singing "I will run when I cannot walk, I will sing when there is no song, I will pray when there is no prayer, I will listen when I cannot hear...I will fight when I cannot feel.[11]"

Through song, I could say openly to the Lord that I felt like I was in the waiting room of silence. I was choosing to run when I didn't feel like getting out of bed. I was making a point to talk when I had no prayers inside me. I was deciding that with each step, I would wait until His silence had ended and He had chosen to respond. Music was giving me a voice to the desperate cries inside.

Step after step, I beat the pavement with my legs, weeping and asking God, "How long will you hide from me? How long will this last?"

Verse after verse, I shouted *"He has torn us into pieces, He has injured us, come let us return to the Lord. He will heal us, He will bandage our wounds, in just a short time, He'll restore us. In just a short time, He'll restore His church so we*

---

[11] **Waiting Room** *by Shane Barnard Psalms Album*

might live, we might live in His presence. Oh that we might know the Lord, let us press on to know Him. Then as surely as the coming of the dawn. He will respond.[12]"

I can't imagine what the neighbors thought of me. They had to have wondered if the death of our son had finally sent me over the edge. I was like one of those people you see at the grocery store when you think they are talking to themselves but then you get close and realize they are talking on some small gadget attached to their ear. That was me, running up and down the street, looking like a crazed woman talking to herself. Only I wasn't talking to myself. I was crying out to the only One who could help.

These songs, these Scriptures rolling around in my head each day is what changed me. These prayers and cries offered up to God began to heal my heart. The words repeated over and over that "HE WILL RESPOND" gave me hope. Yes, I was torn to pieces, I was injured, but He promises to restore us. These words did just what God said they would do; they transformed me.

---

[12] Hosea by Shane Barnard Psalms Album

I now firmly believe that one of the key factors in God healing my heart was praise and worship. Yes, we are to live a life of worship in everything we do, but I am specifically talking about praise and worship through music. These hymns played over and over in my head changed my heart... These Scriptures set to music transformed my thinking.

My dear friend who experienced the heartbreak of the death of her sweet daddy blogged about what music was getting her through her dark places. She called it her "top ten survival playlist."

Not long after, I wrote my own top ten survival playlist and gave it to her along with an Itunes and Starbucks gift card. Many people ask me how to help someone when they are going through a loss. My answer? Music and some Starbucks coffee can bring a temporary, although fleeting, dose of joy.

Early in our marriage, it wasn't like this for me. I was married to a worship leader but never really "got it" until Jake died. Brad could spend hours just playing his guitar and singing to the Lord and I would often shake my head in wonder at the time and energy he spent playing that guitar. It was like I was an outsider looking in - I couldn't hold a tune and so I just quietly sang during our church worship time, waiting on the sermon to start.

Then Jake died, and worship (I am defining the singing to the Lord as worship here - I know there are many forms of worship) became my lifeline. When I had no words to say to the Lord, the songs gave me a voice. Suddenly, the nights of Brad playing guitar became more than just an activity he did. It became our voice in a silent and crumbling world. I watched as Brad processed his grief through music and knew that I had been missing out on something.

I wanted what he had. There was a release he had found that I knew I needed. Brad introduced me to the sacrifice of worship. What started as an uncomfortable lifting of my hands turned into a freedom to raise my hands to the One who was seeing us through.

What started out as a sacrifice to sing through the tears became a sweet release of emotions that left me feeling full inside. What started out as the beginning of a service became some of the sweetest times in my life. Brad taught me the gift of worshipping God through song.

Not too long ago, Brad was asked to lead worship for a worship night for a local church in town. I was excited to go with him. We drove through an older neighborhood that looked as if it belonged in the historical district. We pulled into a tree lined parking lot to a house that had been turned into a church. We walked into an open foyer and a large room filled with chairs. It was warm and inviting like a fire lit living room, the lights were dim and candles lit the stage.

Brad stood there with just a guitar and a mic and he led us in worship to the Lord. It was a small but loud group, worshipping voices were heard over the guitar. There was a quiet desperation for God to show up. There was the feeling that we would not leave till our hearts had poured out the muddy waters and been filled with His Living Water.

Brad shared a verse that, if I have heard before, I don't remember; and it spoke directly to my heart: "That is what the Lord says, Turn to me now, while there is time. Give me your hearts. Come with fasting, weeping, and mourning. Don't tear your clothing in your grief but tear your hearts instead.' Return to the Lord your God, for he is merciful and compassionate,slow to get angry and filled with unfailing love. He is eager to relent and not punish." (Joel 2: 12-13).

And then we sang this song that Brad had written:

There's no room for them here, All these things I hold dear
Father, take them; come, replace them
I can't keep this inside, Lord, I've nowhere to hide
Father, take them; come replace them

Be the king on the throne, Be the Lord all alone
In my heart, in my heart
Come to rule and to reign, Jesus, have Your own way
In my heart, in my heart
Til there's nothing there but You...be the king of my heart[13]

I left that night full of Jesus. I left having surrendered things in worship that were not of him. I left with Him as king of my heart. I left having spent a few hours on a Saturday night renewing my spirit with His Spirit. I left thankful for my husband, for all the nights he stays up for hours singing and playing his guitar.

I left thankful that leading worship isn't just my husband's job; it is his life. It is who he is - a worshipper. I left thankful I learned from him something that has forever changed my relationship with the Lord. I left knowing that the same act of worship that healed me through the death of Jake would heal me through the mundane chores of the day.

---

[13] Lyrics from King of My Heart by Brad Ewing; © 2011

I left realizing that I needed to take the same amount of time in worship of Him today as I did the weeks after Jake died. I left knowing that worship was more than just some songs to sing - worship was the tool to survival in this life.

One night, our youngest son, Jackson, was very sick. We have all had those kind of nights when we are in a dead sleep and then you hear a blood-curdling scream and then after the scream is the vomiting. The kind that has left a trail of vomit on your carpet from their room to yours.

Poor kid had the stomach bug. He was scared and miserable and just couldn't stop throwing up. I was up washing towels and praying that we wouldn't all get it - AGAIN (this is the second time it has run through our house).

I was wondering how many sleepless nights would occur in our household. Then the sweetest thing happened. After Jackson had gotten sick and I was trying to comfort him back to sleep, he cried out "I just want someone to sing with me." I sort of thought he was maybe just a bit delusional since I don't sing. I replied, "That is your dad's area. I just clean up throw up." Then Brad went downstairs, got his guitar, sat at the end of the couch that Jackson was lying on, and sang to him.

I lay in my bed and watched as he sang "Don't Cry, I Am Home" which was Jackson's request. I almost died right then and there. It was just about the sweetest thing I have ever been a part of. To watch his daddy sing him to sleep. To see his daddy quiet his tears and settle him to sleep.

This was a perfect picture of what God does for us when we are hurting, crying, or distraught, God sings over us. What a picture! He loves us so. Zephaniah 3:17, "The Lord your God is with you, He is mighty to save. He will take great delight in you, He will quiet you with his love, He will rejoice over you with singing."

God will quiet us with His love if we allow Him to do it. We can rest against His chest calmly as the Psalmist wrote. We can let our Heavenly Father quiet our hearts even when our hearts are full of questions and doubts. He can and will quiet us with His love.

CHAPTER FOURTEEN
UNCERTAIN

Sometimes, the uncertainty of life slams you in the face. It is almost as if you don't want to do anything or commit to anything because you know that life can unfortunately change in an instant. Life is never certain, but that is never more of a reality than when you have faced an unexpected loss.

For the longest time I would not even allow Brad to turn the car on unless we were all in the car with our seat belts on. If I heard the car turn on and Drew was not in his seat, I would have a surge of fear that would race through my body. I could not calm down until we were all buckled in. Things that once seemed so mundane can now cause me fear.

I'm learning that the only way to combat this is to look to the One who never changes.

Maybe your life has changed. He hasn't. Stand on the promise that God is the same yesterday, today, and forever. This will change how you feel about everything.

I began to see the world through the reality of life and death, and the things that people worried about seemed to trivial. This is very difficult in friendships. Most of my friends were happily discussing diaper bags, mom's day out, and pregnancy weight.

I was busy having an ongoing discussion with God about death. It put me on a different plane than most folks, and I didn't really know how to get back into their world. Partly because I didn't fit into their world and partly because it just hurt too much to see the widening gap between us.

I felt I had aged twenty years in a few months, and those around me just couldn't relate. They tried, and I will always love them for the gap they tried to close, but they were all having babies and changing diapers. I had buried my baby and was changing plants at a grave site.

I was in my early twenties and spent many of my afternoons in counseling sessions instead of putting my two year old down for an afternoon nap. I was no longer forced to go home for nap time; I had all the time in the world.

I had too much time. For a mom whose days had been filled chasing a two year and five year old, the days seemed emptier with just one child.

I also felt awkward everywhere I went. I felt like the general population was almost scared of me, as if I were contagious. They wanted to see me, how I was reacting, how I was doing, but they never wanted to get too close.

One day I went to a Bible study for the first time since the accident. The registration form they asked me to fill out asked how many kids I had. I didn't know how to answer that, so I got up crying and left with tears in my eyes.

I felt like Job did when he said "He has removed my brothers far from me, and my acquaintances are completely estranged from me. My relatives have failed, and my close friends have forgotten me[14]."

The months after I lost Jake were the loneliest times for me. Not because my friends and family didn't try. One day we were at Brad's office with another one of Brad's best friends, Matt. He was sitting behind his desk, and we all began to talk about Jake. He didn't say anything eloquent or try to explain; a few tears just rolled down his eyes.

Matt, a six-three, 240 pound man sat behind his desk with light streaming in from the window and softly cried for us. We didn't say anything but stood there and cried. It was a tender time for everyone.

---

[14] Job 19:13-14

It must have been awkward to be our friends during this time. People wanted to help and to fix it, but it just couldn't be fixed with human hands or words. Friendships alone couldn't fix what was wrong with me. Only Jesus can fix our shattered hearts.

My heart was in a million pieces, and human touch couldn't piece me back together - not my preacher father, not my husband, not even Beth Moore. I knew they couldn't, and thankfully I never made them try. All too often I think we look to people and things to make us feel better, and there is just no way they can.

Everyday conversations were a nightmare for me. Normal questions that people ask became difficult to answer. "How many kids do you have?" was a question that I dreaded. If I answered "Two," they wanted to know ages and then I had to explain. If I answered one when Drew was around, he took it as a personal assault against his brother and proceeded to shout to the world that we in fact had two kids and that his brother was in heaven.

It was just too much. I began to shy away from those conversations, and I made sure I was never in a room where some one might ask me that. I never wanted to talk about myself. I didn't want to have to explain. It was just too hard.

Friendships are hard no matter what. Just like in Job, friends can unintentionally make the grief worse. "Friendship didn't offer Job much consolation when his world collapsed around him. He thought God was his friend, but his losses cast a shadow over God's goodness and justice.

How could years of faithfulness to God add up to this? His closest friends suspected Job was hiding a scandal. Surely he deserved God's punishment for something he'd done wrong — some secret sin he had locked away in his closet to preserve his untarnished image[15]."

I think it is easier for people to look at a tragic situation and immediately find fault with the person. It makes the tragedy easier to swallow when we can blame someone. It is much harder to work through tragedy when there is no human fault.

Job's friends were constantly trying to find fault with Job in order to explain away the tragedy. They wanted something to pin it on so that they could possibly thwart that tragedy from happening to them. We all do this, don't we? In the end, we are

---

[15] The Gospel of Ruth: Loving God Enough to Break the Rules (Carolyn Custis James)

seeking a way to control or explain away the difficulties in our lives. We think that if we follow a set of rules, we will get a certain result.

When tragedy occurs and there is no one to blame, there are questions that we aren't too sure we can answer or we just don't want to know the answer. Right after our accident, a friend was telling me how scared she was with her car and around her kids. She said she kept telling her husband and kids over and over to be careful. Eventually her husband looked at her and said, "Don't you think Brad and Kasey were careful? It was an accident we all have to live with."

Do you understand the root of her fears? It comes down to control. We think if we can just control each aspect of our lives, bad things won't happen; or if we don't do this or that, we can prevent tragedy. I am not saying to live recklessly. I am saying that there will be things in this life that we can't prevent no matter how many precautions we take, no matter how many warnings we heed, no matter how many prayers we pray.

When your life feels out of control, when events change your expected outcome, how are you going to react? When there is no one to blame, how do you handle the why's that rise up from within?

There comes that moment in time when we must get face to face with the One who we know could have changed the outcome but didn't. I had to accept that God could have prevented the accident but He didn't.

I had to face head on the question that lingered in the back of my mind. Why did God allow this to happen and not prevent it? I knew that a powerful, Almighty God could have changed the outcome of that tragic Sunday, yet He didn't. That question still danced around in my soul but I wasn't ready to give voice to the most perplexing question of all time. WHY?

CHAPTER FIFTEEN
SELF PRESERVATION

I think one of the hardest parts of grief is having to absorb the pain of the loss and deal with your own character at the same time. Pain increases our awareness of things around us, and we must deal with our selfishness, disobedience, and sin all the while we are hurting in the most awful of ways.

I don't know if we expect to be given a free pass to act how we want because of the tragedy we face, but I think we can get used to the special treatment we are given and resent others when they stop giving it.

A tragedy can bring a certain amount of attention, and we as humans like attention. When a new tragedy occurs that no longer has to do with us and someone else becomes the object of attention, we long for the status we once had. How we deal with this can affect our whole lives.

We can quickly become bitter. We can be upset that we were forced into the unwanted role of the grieving mother and then become disheartened when we have been dethroned for the next big story. And a bigger story will come, leaving you feeling confused. Leaving you to wonder what you did to lose all of the love and concern.

May I offer a warning here for you? Grief can be selfish.

Phillip Yancey says, "Pain narrows vision, the most private of sensations, it forces us to think of ourselves and little else." We can go quickly from taking time for ourselves to heal to total self preservation. The line is subtle and sometimes hard to find, but you must work with the Spirit to ensure you don't cross it. I can't tell you your line, but I can tell you that Satan wants you to cross it and will tempt you at every turn. He would be happy for you to become inwardly focused; content to deal with your own grief so that you never look up again.

Please hear me on this; it is important to take time to heal. But it is also important that as you heal, you look outside yourself. If it is always about you and what you suffered, you might need to take some time with the Father to ask Him to adjust your heart.

There has to come a point in your life when it is no longer about you and what has happened to you but about Him and what He is doing through you. Selfishness can creep up before we know it and we must fight it.

There are often times when I have to have my own "heart check" before the Lord. I have to say to God, "I want this to be about me today, and I know it is not. Lord, can you please change my heart on this?" I have learned a little trick here that can be done anywhere. I breathe out, and I tell the Lord I am breathing out me; and as I breathe in, will you please breathe Yourself into me? I do this repeatedly until I feel like I have given over thoughts of myself and my hurt and I am filled with Him.

Honestly, there are still some very difficult days when I miss Jake so very much. Of course, anniversaries and holidays are hard and cause me to miss him, but there are days that take me by surprise. I see a toddler that reminds me of him, and it can take my breathe away. Or when school starts and I think of what year in school he should be attending.

There are days when I have to walk into a hospital or sit through a funeral where I just want everyone to feel my hurt all over again. The first time I stepped foot into a hospital after Jake's death was difficult. A friend of mine had a two-year old with cancer and he was having tests, so I went to see them at the hospital. I walked into the room, her son popped up out of the bed with this tiny white gown on, and I was momentarily frozen.

Memories flooded back of Jake lying on the hospital bed that Sunday afternoon. I teared up a bit, and my friend understood that it was difficult for me; but I left knowing I had accomplished a trip to the hospital and that the next time would be a little easier.

Just a few weeks ago, I was standing at my sink washing dishes when Jackson ran in and said the neighbor was hit by a car. (He is okay; he is home with his mom right now with only bumps and bruises). I ran out after Jackson, crossing the street to the neighbor's front yard to find a sweet mom in the grass holding her baby boy. He was crying but thankfully, coherent. He looked scraped and bruised but otherwise okay. I moved into action mode, called 911, got the witnesses, talked to the police, and took care of the older boys.

Once all the chaos settled down and all the boys were taken care of, I calmly walked back to my room and locked my door. I was shaking all over and trying to catch my breath as I was assaulted with memories.

Doubt and fear ravaged the outer layer of my heart, moving quickly toward full-blown panic. I ran a bath, allowing the warm water to calm the outside, but the water did nothing for the questions clamoring to be answered. "Why?" rang out so loudly in my head I couldn't fight it. It begged to be asked, again and again, Why? Why? Why? Why did Jake have to die?

I am learning to put a voice to that question that lingers in my soul, to be a bit more like Job who looked for God, the one he knew had the answers. I am learning to plead my case.

He didn't answer my questions, but He listened and eventually settled my heart. I was thankful for my memory verse, reminding me that I needed Him to fill my heart with His peace and not allow it to be filled with doubt. Romans 15:13 "May the God of hope fill you with all joy and peace as you trust in him, so that you may overflow with hope by the power of the Holy Spirit."

He did just that.

He was enough.

Doubt and fear receded.

Peace overflowed.

CHAPTER SIXTEEN
HE'S NOT SAFE, BUT HE'S GOOD

Our pastor, Fred Lowery, often says to the congregation, "God is good" and we respond, "All the time." He replies, "All the time" and we respond with, "God is good." Why do we repeat this together? We do it so that we understand deep down in our souls that God is truly good. This is something we are practicing in the light before the darkness comes. When darkness hits, we react knowing that, "God is good, all the time. All the time, God is good."

I love these lines from C.S. Lewis' famous book, The Lion, the Witch and the Wardrobe. The following conversation about Aslan takes place between Susan and Mr. and Mrs. Beaver.

"Is he quite safe? I shall feel rather nervous about meeting a lion."

"That you will dearie, and no mistake," said Mrs. Beaver. "If there's anyone who can appear before Aslan without their knees knocking, they're either braver than most or just plain silly."

"Then he isn't safe?" said Lucy.

"Safe?" said Mr. Beaver; "don't you hear what Mrs. Beaver tells you? Who said anything about safe? Of course he isn't safe. But he's good. He's the King, I tell you."

We must know that the Christian life isn't necessarily safe and won't be trouble-free, but God is good. We can know that in the end, it will be worth it. Jesus does not take all the pain and heartache away from us; He makes it worth it. He gives our hurts purpose.

 I have five boxes sitting in my car. I have peeked in at their contents but don't have the nerve to go through them yet. Right after Jake died, friends and family just packed up our house for us since we never went back there ourselves. The accident happened at our house. We didn't want to go back.

 My cousin has stored these boxes in her attic since then. They are moving, so she called me one night and said that she found boxes of Jake's stuff. I teared up a bit and asked what was in the boxes.

 His toys, his backpack - the one he took to preschool each day, some clothes, you know, boy stuff. Brad and I picked up the boxes, and they are still sitting in the back of my car. I see them in my rearview mirror, but I avoid the inevitable and keep driving around with a car full of stuff.

 I peeked in and saw items that my Jake used to hold. I took another glance and saw a backpack that he carried so proudly as he walked into his preschool room. I closed up the box tightly; some things just hurt too much to open. I want to see it, but then

I don't. So I go on, driving around town looking like I am the one moving.

In these last few weeks, I have had dear friends who have had their lives interrupted by pain. Not the death kind of pain, but the life kind of pain. We all experience it; we are going about our lives, and suddenly an event happens that shakes us to the core. The kind of pain resulting from living in a fallen world. Often, we can deny the pain and keep the box closed, but some events just force the box wide open and we must come into contact with the pain and sin of this world. It hurts, and we hurt; and we are left sitting around looking at life and wondering why "this" had to happen.

In our small group, we are going through David Platt's Old Testament Survey, and he said something that jumped out to me. "It is not in our successes that we grow closer to God but in our pain." He also said that pain is a privilege because it is what God uses to draw us to Him. I have often considered writing a book called "The Privilege of Pain." I don't know much, but I know that to be true - that God uses our pain to draw us closer to Him.

On my run this morning, my prayer list was long. So many are hurting, but I was reminded to be thankful for the pain in my life and the pain in the life of my friends. The heartbreaking struggles we face really are a gift from God. A life lived without trouble or trials is sure to result a life lived away from the presence of God.

Instead of ignoring those boxes in my car, I am going to get them out and bring them in. I am going to open the painful parts of my heart and let Him use that anguish to draw me closer to Him.

It must be ingrained deep down that God is for us and not against us. The eighth chapter of Romans states that, "All things will work together for good for those who love Him and are called according to His purposes." When that truth has penetrated our hearts we will react differently to situations.

When tragedy strikes, we can stand on the promise that God will work all things together for good. We pour theology, the study of who God is, into our hearts when life is good; and then when the storms hit, we draw from that prior knowledge.

We need to force ourselves to know Him more when life is easy and doesn't require our complete dependence on God. We need to study His Word and then study His Word some more. We need to be in a church that preaches the Word of God fully. We need to be convicted by it, comforted by it, and work on a more complete knowledge of it.

Study Him like you are pursuing a doctorate in God. When circumstances are seen from the mountain of who God is, they seem much smaller.

Is there hope for those who haven't been steeped in God's Word? Yes, there is hope, but the road to recovery might be rockier. If this is the case with you, surround yourself immediately with other people who have a deep history with God. Allow their knowledge and intimacy with God to spill out into your life. Use them and their knowledge of the holy to help transform your way of thinking about who God is and how you can walk through difficult times relying on Him. That's certainly what my friend Ginger did for me.

Don't refuse the things you know you should do because they are hard. Resist the urge to numb the pain with things other than God. After Jake's death we had to face so many hard things. It was easier to look away, be angry, work, run, or cry, but at the end of the day, in the quiet of the night we had a choice, run from Him or to Him.

CHAPTER SEVENTEEN
WAITING AND BLESSINGS

Brad wrote a song called "In the Meantime" a few months after Jake died. This song describes perfectly how we were living then and how we have to live now.

Lord I don't understand what you are doing with me,
I don't have a clue
How I wish that you would let me see, see what you are up to
But if you don't, I pray this simple prayer, and lift it to you
Would you hold me tight and tell me that you care
And hold me here in the meantime

Though our son has been gone for a little while,
We still feel the pain
Though we're aching to see his precious smile,
We'll see it one day

As we wait, we pray this simple prayer, Jesus to You
Would you hold him tight and tell him that we care,
And hold us here in the meantime

As were learning to live with joy and pain, with you by our side
We can climb all the mountains and endure the rain
As we run for the prize

And Jesus, as we yearn for your kingdom now,
Teach us to wait
Fill our hearts with hope, and show us how
How to live in the meantime

That, my friends, is exactly what we had to do, live in the meantime. We longed to be with Jake; we longed for Jesus to come back, but we had to figure out what to do with ourselves until that day came. We continued to live with Brad's parents, and slowly Brad began looking for a job.

This was a painful process: we were raw and hurting but desperate to settle down somewhere. Our lives were on hold, and we were living in limbo. Drew was supposed to start pre-school and we just couldn't let him go. I wasn't ready for him to be out of my sight. The thought of dropping Drew off with anyone but my parents was too much for me. I wanted him with me all the time.

I still clung to the verses about God's plan and purpose for us. Jeremiah 29:11 is still one of my go to verses "For I know the plans I have for you, declares the LORD, plans for welfare and not for evil, to give you a future and a hope."

I prayed that good would come out of this tragedy. I didn't want good for others; I wanted it for us, for Drew, Brad and me. I wanted happy, easy contentment, not "well with my soul" good. I had to let God change my definition of good.

Good doesn't mean easy.

Ephesians 2:10 says "For we are his workmanship, created in Christ Jesus for good works, which God prepared beforehand, that we should walk in them." The Greek word for workmanship is *poiema,* which literally means "'a thing made'; it comes into English as poem. The word indicates a handiwork, a masterpiece. God's church is His 'poem,' His masterpiece."[16]

We are God's masterpiece, and if we work with Him, He is creating a story with our lives that will reveal Him to others. His plans for us are for our good, but they are also for the good of others. Our purpose, our plan here on this earth, is to be a mouthpiece that draws others to Him.

We eventually accepted an offer at a small church in Colorado Springs, Colorado. We moved in the beginning August, 2002, almost one year after Jake's death. Until this point, we had been surrounded by family and friends.

Our move to Colorado rocked our comfort zone and our stability. We now had to learn how to be a family without Jake here on this earth. We had been surrounded by so many people that we didn't know how to live together, just the three of us. There were awkward silences, long dinners, and hard adjustments. We did it though. We pressed on, and we began to be a family again.

---

[16] Nelson's New Illustrated Bible Commentary "workmanship"

Drew started kindergarden and had a hard time. He couldn't keep still; he wouldn't sit with his legs crossed; he didn't do "this"; he did "that" instead. The teacher wanted to talk to me everyday. Nonsense.

I dreaded picking him up. We both cried a lot. He was struggling in school, and I was struggling without him. Finally, we decided that we should homeschool him and give him one more year of recovery. I met a lady at our church who offered to tutor him, and she was a miracle worker. She had that boy reading and loving it in no time. We were finally beginning to see the light at the end of the tunnel.

Deep inside, I began to long for another baby. I knew this was impossible because I had had my tubes tied after Jake was born, but I felt like we were not complete. I began praying and researching my options. I searched the internet and found a clinic in Atlanta, Georgia that specialized in tubal reversal surgeries. After much prayer and thought, we decided to give it a try.

My sisters and I all lived in three different states and decided to meet in Atlanta for the surgery. This may sound crazy to you, it sure does to me now as I am writing this. What were we thinking?

I scheduled a huge surgery across the country without even meeting the doctor first! My sister, Angela, said she got a bit nervous when I walked back to the operating room. She began to wonder if we shouldn't have checked this out some more. Oh well, it was too late. I can assure you we have done crazier things before and since.

Soon, I woke up; bright lights dotted the room. Strange faces peered over me. My brain felt hazy, reality slowly presented itself, and I became aware that the surgery was over. The doctor began explaining that the surgery went very well, and according to his tests, it was a success. He gave me a hopeful diagnosis; try for a year to get pregnant, and if you can't, come back and we will try again.

I had assumed it would be difficult, so I had mentally prepared myself for a year-long wait. After all we had been through, I expected the worst.

We left the clinic, rented movies, and went back to our hotel room to settle in for my recovery. I lay in the bed of a worn out hotel room with my two sisters. My body ached all over; I was surprised at how much my insides hurt. I lay there on stiff, white hotel sheets while my sisters catered to my every wish hoping to ease a small amount of the physical pain.

Their presence eased the emotional pain. I was broken from the last year of heartache, and we were silently hoping that the surgery would work and open a door for another baby in our lives.

We watched girly movies that forced us to laugh through our tears. It was a special time for the three of us. It had been a rough year for our family, and I believe God gave us that time to recover together.

That weekend while in Atlanta we were close to where my grandparents lived and we went to see our Pop. He had cancer, and we got to spend the night with him. I remember carefully climbing up into bed with him and just lying next to him. It was the last time I ever saw my Pop.

I am amazed at how God used that time. A surgery needed to fix a careless attempt on my part to control the events of my life allowed my sisters and me to see our Pop one last time.

God is in the details of our lives; He orchestrates the events of our lives just perfectly. Don't ever forget that.

Once I settled in back home, I mentally geared myself up for a year long wait. However, two months after my surgery, I was pregnant!

Then pure terror struck me; I was going to have another baby... all I could think about was what if this child died too. It paralyzed me. What had I done?

Like the Shunammite woman in Second Kings, I wasn't ready to subject myself to the possibilities of a baby.

At our first doctors appointment, we had to have an ultrasound to insure that all was well and there was not a tubal pregnancy, which is common after a reversal surgery.

I dreaded this. I was just waiting for the bad news to come. Once your world has been shattered the way ours had, nothing seems to be solid anymore. Things that you usually wouldn't have even given a second thought to now agonized me. If Drew had a cold, I thought he was dying of pneumonia. If my mom called, I thought something had happened to my dad. If my dad called after 7:00 p.m., I thought something was wrong with my sisters. When the nightmare has occurred, you never relax.

You're always thinking there is another tragedy around the corner.

The ultrasound was good news, and the baby began to progress with no apparent problems. We breathed a small sigh of relief, but inside I still kept gearing up for the next big heartbreak. I just kept fearing that something was going to go wrong.

It never did, except for the fact that I was heavier than I have ever been in my whole life! Kid number three really does a number on your body. I was shocked by the quick weight gain.

I slowly began to enjoy the idea of a new baby. Now we had baby showers instead of funerals. We had happy visits to the hospital planning for our future and not visits ending our dreams. God was beginning to redeem our brokenness. He was bringing in little pieces of light to our dark world.

On October 7, 2003, we had a healthy baby boy, Jackson Paul Ewing. We had a smooth delivery and a happy little boy. I must tell you that Brad redeemed himself from his previous mishap in the delivery room.

Brad did not pass out or throw up once. He kept his color the whole time and was still standing by the time I delivered Jackson Ewing. I was very proud of him, and I was elated about our new baby boy. I could see that God was redeeming more than just a father in a delivery room; he was redeeming our lives.

Then I had to go home from the hospital. Every time he cried, I thought he was sick. If he spit up, I was ready to take him to the emergency room. I couldn't relax. I finally cried out to God. I can't live this way. He gently whispered to me, "I know; you were never intended to live like this. You were intended to trust Me." I did, but it was hard. Very hard.

I was having to learn a new relationship with God. A relationship that had been through the wringer. I was learning how to relax in the every day hustle and bustle of life. The desperation to make it through the day had worn off, and now I was having to figure out how to keep my relationship with Him intimate.

The stinging pain was not so constant. I enjoyed those times of pain-free living, yet I was still plagued with those nagging thoughts of "What if?"

There was something in the back of my mind that couldn't rest. It was as if I was on pins and needles waiting for the next disaster to strike. I tarried between fear and safety, anxiety and peace.

Pain can be a drug of sorts. You get so used to feeling it that the second it seems to lessen, you are in a type of withdrawal.

I had lived for a year with a constant ache, and now God was teaching me how to love Him in the calm of my day, not just in the dark of the night. That poem I had read so long ago in a hot bath was happening to me.

...I offered Him my future, and released to Him my past.
I traded in my dreams, for a plan He said would last.

CHAPTER EIGHTEEN
INTRODUCING JOB

I didn't even make the connection until I went back and reread the poem that I had been reading in the bathtub right before Jake's death. My prayer had been for me to have the kind of faith that doesn't require evidence; to trust, regardless of the situation; to believe when I couldn't "see" His plan.

My prayer had been just that, to be a woman who walks by faith and not by sight. I had had no idea what God was preparing me for when I offered up that prayer, but He knew. He was softening my heart, giving me a tender example of what a Lord can do in the midst of great tragedy if I would trust Him.

I can't tell you how grateful I am that He orchestrated my path so that my heart would be soft enough to listen to Him and my walk would be strong enough to endure the storms ahead.

I could weep for joy as I sit here typing out how God engineered the events and people in my life before Jake's death forcing me to build my life on Him. I was forced to hear His words and listen. Then, when the torrential rains came and the floods threatened to destroy us, I was still standing.

You have to know the story of Job to get the full meaning of what that one prayer in the bathtub continues to do in my life. Job was a man who God says was "a servant, none like him on the earth, blameless and upright, who fears God and turns away from evil." (Job 1:8) And what does Job get for his integrity, for his blameless and upright heart? God brags on Job.

Satan says to God, "Does Job fear God for no reason? Have you not put a hedge around him and his house and all that he has, on every side? You have blessed the work of his hands, and his possessions have increased in the land. But stretch out your hand and touch all that he has, and he will curse you to your face." (Job 1:10-11)

God responds to Satan by giving him permission to take from Job "all that he has is in your hand, only against him, do not stretch out your hand." (1:12) Satan unleashes his venom and kills his servants, his oxen, donkeys, sheep, camels, his sons and his daughters, all in the same moment!

Job responds to these horrific tragedies by tearing his robe, shaving his head (ancient mourning practices) and falling on the ground worshipping and crying out to God, "Naked I came from my mothers womb, and naked I shall return. The

Lord gave, and the Lord has taken away; blessed be the name of the Lord." (1:21)

Don't miss the weight of everything that Job lost on that day. Go to Job 1:13-19 and carefully read what kind of day Job had. He lost all his worldly possessions and his children *at the same time*.

Yet, "In all this Job did not sin or charge God with wrong." (1:22) How often do we charge God with wrong for so many things that happen to us? Is our first response to God when something is taken away from us to bless God because He is the one who gives and takes away?

I know that mine is not. One thing Job knew that we must learn is that God's dealings with us are never wrong.

Hard to understand? Yes! Wrong? Never!

The beginning of chapter two of Job says "Again there was a day when the sons of God came to present themselves before the Lord, and Satan also came among them to present himself before the Lord."

On a side note, I think it is funny (not really funny, but comical) that Satan presents himself to the Lord. Satan presents himself before the Lord, just as the sons of God stand ready to present themselves to God. It sure looks as if God is showing us a glimpse of His authority in heaven. The Hebrew word for "present themselves" is used for the angels presenting themselves to God,[17] and the word is also used to mean "to stand ready for service to authority, as a function of worship, implying subservience and submission"[18].

Satan might have presented himself before the Lord with the sole purpose of wreaking havoc on Job's life but let's not miss this here - God had His own purposes for what He was going to do. While Satan thought he would show God that Job only loves Him for His blessing, God shows us how His purposes are not thwarted by man or Satan. God will accomplish what He sets out to accomplish. Period.

Satan, after presenting himself to the Lord, realizes that Job has not responded the way that he first thought. So, Satan responds again with his less than creative answer, "Skin for Skin! All that a man has he will give for his life. But stretch out your hand and touch his bones and his flesh and he will curse you to your face."

---

[17] Gesenius' Hebrew-Chaldee Lexicon of OT

[18] Dictionary of Biblical Languages with Semantic Domains

God again gives Satan permission to take his health but not his life. Satan strikes Job with sores all over his body. They are so bad that Job takes broken pottery to scrape himself with while sitting in ashes. Job has reached a new low, and to top it off, his wife tells him to curse God and die.

Now that the second shoe has dropped, how does Job respond? He says, "Shall we receive good from God, and shall we not receive evil?". And in ALL of this Job did not sin with his lips (v.9).

I pray for a heart like Job. A heart that loves God for who He is and not what He does.

CHAPTER NINETEEN
STRUGGLE WELL

I think the book of Job is the perfect book for those struggling with grief. Job shows us how to grieve. He gives us an example we can all glean from. Job questions, doubts, trusts, believes, and even longs for his own death.

He struggles. We can surely relate to that, but he offers hope as well.

A few years ago, I spoke at a women's event in Mobile, Alabama. It was the same church that helped me grow closer to God in college. I walked through the same doors I had walked through so many times to learn more about Jesus, but this particular time I was there to share with these ladies all that God had done in my life. Talk about a turn around!

What an amazing God we serve. He took a bitter, pregnant, nineteen year old college student and through the change that only Jesus can do in a life, I can now tell of the goodness of the Lord.

By God's grace, I was able to show those ladies, many who knew me as the pregnant pastor's daughter, what God can do. He came here to save the lost and the sinners, of which I was one of the greatest.

I received a letter from a young college girl, and she went on for pages with the heartache she was fighting. My heart went out to her. She ended her letter with two words, "struggling well." That, my friend, is what we do. When all is said and done, may it be said of us that we did struggle, but we struggled well! Brad and I struggled with the loss of Jake. We struggled well and not so well sometimes, but we learned so much about who God is. Grief made us honest with ourselves and with our God.

I can get confused by the fact that God says that Job didn't sin with his mouth, but we see him complain to God about his situation. Verse after verse Job asks for an audience with the Lord so that he can understand what is going on with his life.

Look in the middle of Job and you will also see a man who was heartbroken and often cried out to God. He cried out for rescue, for peace, and for relief. God shows us it is alright to cry out to Him from the depths of our hurts and our lack of faith.

Yes, we are given the freedom to vent, but we are also given a context in which to do it. That is why the Psalms can be so beneficial to us as believers. We can use the very Psalms that other Christians have used for years to cry out to God. God has given us permission to cry out to Him, and He has given us the very words with which to speak. For those of us who are too weak and hurt too much to speak, God's word can speak for us.

One book Brad particularly loved was called "Lament for a Son" by Nicholas Wolterstorff. It offered pages of his deepest heart's cry right there in black and white. Some of them are truly scary to read.

The emotions one feels at the loss of a child can be a dangerous wonder to see written on a page. I even hesitated to add my journal due to the sheer nature of the anger, frustration, and hopelessness I sometimes felt.

According to Wolterstorff, "Lament is the language of suffering, the voicing of suffering...Lament is an achievement. Lament is more, though, than the voicing of suffering. The mere voicing of one's suffering is complaint, not lament. Lament is a cry to God. This presupposes, of course, that lament is the action of a believer."

Lamenting is what I did while running and pouring my heart out to God. Lamenting is using the Psalms to vent your anger, frustration, or lack of understanding for the situations you have found yourself in.

Lamenting is allowing the grief inside of you to have a voice. You must find your voice. When dealing with grief, you must find an appropriate way to let it out. Read Lamentations. God has given us a guide, a model of how to vent our fears and frustrations.

He has been so kind as to give us words for the hurts we feel. I often feel as if I have no words, but when I am at a loss, He gives me a way to voice the hurt inside.

The Psalms, Job, and Lamentations show us it is okay to cry out when what we know about God seems different than what we are seeing in our present circumstances. One pastor reminded me that God will not fall off His throne if I have questions. He is gracious enough to walk us through our laments.

Appendix 2 at the end of this book I have included more entries from my prayer journal (laments) during the loss of our son. It's painful, honest, and vulnerable, but I hope it gives insight to the grief and struggle of my heart during this time. I also pray that it encourages you to pray honestly and simply to God in your own struggles.

We will all struggle with different events, sicknesses, cancer, and heartbreak here on this earth. Struggle, my friend, but struggle well.

CHAPTER TWENTY
WALLS

After Jake died, a dangerous shift occurred in me. I think that only those that know me really well ever saw the change because I pretended well. I said the right things, looked sad when needed, and paid attention to other children when necessary, but I didn't get emotionally involved with them.

No way. I was surrounded by many people I loved and wouldn't quit loving, but as much as I could control, I wouldn't allow new possible hurts either.

That's what people were to me now, so I shut myself off mentally. I hurt, and I didn't ever want to feel that kind of pain again. Somewhere deep down, I really thought that if I just stopped feeling, I might stop hurting. I had constructed a wall, or maybe even a fortress, around my heart.

Grief is a process, and it takes time. I could have never healed from all that happened to us at once.

When I was little, I hopped on a motorcycle that was still warm from a recent ride. I didn't realize it, but I burned a large part of my leg. It took weeks and many doctor visits for that to heal. There is still a faint mark left on my skin.

At first, the burn had to be covered so that even air couldn't get to it. I had to take extreme care of it; then later I had to put a smaller bandage on it. Then I had to let it get air for a little while and then move to more air every day.

Soon a band-aid was all that I needed. Next, I could walk without any covering on my leg at all. It became a large scab, then a scar, and then just a faint mark.

That is the way God heals us. At first we have to be completely covered, not letting anything in. Then, slowly, God allows a little air to hit our wounds. Then He gently exposes us more and more. God doesn't totally cover us or completely shield us, He gently heals layers one at a time.

I had resurrected some of my old walls in my own way of dealing with the tragedy. But I could feel God gently stripping away at my wall; God didn't allow the walls to totally shield me.

Remember the terror I felt when I found out I was pregnant with Jackson? Less than two years after Jake's death, I was going to have another little boy. I was scared to love him, yet I couldn't help myself.

Jackson is the kind of boy who demands that you love him with everything you have. He wants your full attention and affection. He accepts nothing less. Jackson was just what I needed to force me to feel again.

The choice wasn't up to me; Jackson insisted on and received my full heart. He was just too wonderful for me to withhold my affection. When I would get eye level with him to give him "a talkin' to," he would calmly comb my hair with his fingers and look at me directly in the eyes, as if he was the one calming me.

God has faithfully allowed every layer of my defenses to gradually be brought into the light and air to heal.

Our family has moved into a low income neighborhood in hopes of shining His light on a dark place. Each day I open my home to child after child that needs love and affection. I am beginning to see that as I open myself to others, they help to heal my heart even more.

As I pour out His love to each child, He pours His love into me. Each kid that hugs on me, tells me I smell good, asks to come home with me, or begs for my complete attention shows me a glimpse of His light into my dark heart. Daily interaction with children that need love and attention has shown me that shielding myself is not the answer. Exposure is.

I realize now that on the metal table where Jake's lifeless body lay so many years ago, I lay down with him. I let my emotions die with him that day. Now, the power that raised Jesus from the grave is slowly resurrecting me as well.

CHAPTER TWENTY ONE
WHY VS. WHO

There was plenty of opportunity for God to answer Job but God remained silent. God could have told Job that he was being tested and that He had, in fact, suggested to Satan that Job would pass his test. God could have told him why but chose not to answer his questions.

I feel for Job here. He has spent forty chapters wanting to argue his case before God; and then when God responds, he immediately understands just WHO he was up against. God's patience with us allows our questions, but there comes a time when He asks us questions of His own.

The gravity of God actually answering us is terrifying. What if God actually replied to us while we are flinging our insults toward heaven? It would knock us on our knees, and our faces would fall to the ground. Can you imagine if He began asking us the questions He asked Job?

Here are a few . . .

"Where were you when I laid the foundation of the earth?"
"Who determined the measurements?"
"Or who shut in the sea with doors when it burst out form the womb, when I made clouds its garment and thick darkness its

swaddling band, and prescribed limits for it and set bars and doors, and said, "Thus far you come, and no farther, and here shall your proud waves be stayed?"[19]

Question after question, God is revealing to Job how much He is in control of every aspect that makes the world go round. I think God was answering Job's questions without giving a specific answer. His only answer that He offered Job was not the "Why? but the "Who!"

God's questions answered Job by saying, I am Lord and I can be trusted. Maybe God is asking you the same questions. Will you trust Him with His answers?

Job had no idea what God's plans or purposes were for him and he had to come to terms with just that, that God's plans and purposes for us are too wonderful for us to grasp. We can't attain them. We must trust in who He is, that is the only reasonable response.

Eventually, all the questions of "why" will begin to fade into "Who." We need to ask, "Who are You, God?" That, my friends, will be the only thing that will get you through your trials. That is what will sustain you in the darkest of night. Him.

---

[19] Job 38:4-5,8-12

He is it. He is the only answer. Nothing else will do. Nothing else will satisfy the deepest questions of our being. We must trust Him.

Remember how Ginger ended that first letter to me:

Oh, Kasey I wish I had magic words or formulas, but I don't. I just give you JESUS ...... and HE is enough.

My first reaction to this letter was an instant let-down. You see, I wanted the magic formula to heal my heart. I appreciated the words and cherished them, but I wanted five steps to heal a shattered heart. I wanted an easy fix, and after reading her letter, I realized that there was no easy fix.

Just like Job, I wanted answers. Job never got the answers he was asking for, but Job did get the most important thing. He got God. Eventually, I did too.

It was a slow process, my understanding that God was enough for my heartbreak. It didn't come to me in one crashing moment of revelation. It was a daily fight I had to win in order to see God in all the circumstances. It was a fight to see that God is truly good when I hurt so badly. But as days turned into months, and months turned into years, I realized that God had truly walked me through the valley of the shadow of death and healed my heart.

Some of my favorite verses are in chapter forty two of Job. After God had asked Job all the questions, Job got the "Who" of God. In verse 2 he responds by saying:

Then Job replied to the LORD: "I know that you can do all things; no purpose of yours can be thwarted.

The Hebrew word for 'thwarted' means "be impossible, i.e., be thwarted from a successful solution or to fortify, i.e., strengthen a defensive structure[20]." This definition shows us that God's plans will not be hindered from a successful solution in your life. The things that we think will drag us down the farthest can be the things that God will use to produce the most fruit in our lives.

Our God is able to take whatever mess we make of our lives, whatever evil is thrust upon us, or whatever sin we repent of and use it for His purpose. That is the God we serve. A mighty and awesome God. The magnitude of the reality that God's purposes will be accomplished should bring instant peace to our hearts.

Let that sweep over you for a minute.

---

[20] Dictionary of Biblical Languages with Semamtic Domains: Hebrew (Old Testament) 1307

Nothing, I mean nothing, that has or will ever happen in your life, can't be used by God. No matter what, His purposes can be accomplished in your life. There is one catch though, you have to let Him.

A willing heart is all He asks of us. We must be willing to let Him do His work. Yes, we struggle, but we struggle well. When we struggle well with Him, we open the door for His purposes to be accomplished. "Job, seeing himself in the light of the presence of God, realizes that God permitted him to suffer[21]."

Job came to the conclusion that part of God's purpose for him was to suffer for Him, but it was not suffering for the sake of suffering. He suffered according to God's plan. That makes all the difference.

Verses *three and five say,*

You asked, 'Who is this that obscures my plans without knowledge?' Surely I spoke of things I did not understand, things too wonderful for me to know...I had heard of you by the hearing of the ear, but now my eye sees you.

Job had been questioning things "too wonderful" for him to know. The Hebrew word for 'know' implies more than a grasp

---

[21] Warren Wiersbe

of information; it suggests intimate knowledge of the sort that comes by personal experience. Job realized that he had heard of God by the hearing of the ear, but now he was beginning to know Him on a more intimate level. In his suffering, Job was experiencing God in ways he had never imagined. He understood that what was happening to him was much bigger than what he could see directly in front of him.

While Job was definitely going through some growing pains in his walk with God, I can't help but think that Job's previous knowledge of God was a foundation to stand upon in his own trials.

We can't discount our pursuit of spiritual growth in the calm days. It will anchor us in the eye of our own storm that is bound to come. The things we hear and learn in the light will be the things that sustain us in the dark.

It causes me to think about my own upbringing. I'm so grateful for my parents and the church. Over the course of my life I had been taught the goodness of God. My dad always says "When you can't see His hand, trust His heart."

It was easier for me to trust God's heart in my own darkness because I had been taught about God and His character.

I knew from previous experiences that we could walk in the deep of the night and see the sun rise the next morning.

We so often ease up on our relationship with God when life is good. We don't press in quite as hard. We don't dig deep to discover more of His timeless truths. If you take away one thing from this book, take this..dig deeper, study harder, memorize Scripture.

Do the hard work, and I promise you, when the dead of night frightens you to the core of your being, you will have a deep and abiding peace that passes all understanding. Like Job, you will be able to say, "Now, my eyes have seen you."

When we begin to see God, we are satisfied with who He is, and all the "whys" seem to take a backseat to what is important. Phillip Yancey says "A person who lives in faith must proceed on incomplete evidence, trusting in advance what will only make sense in reverse." Amen!

I am about to jump out of my chair reveling and remembering what God has done. Remember my prayer all those years ago in the bathtub? To walk by faith, not by sight.

God answered that prayer completely. Yes, there were years we had to walk by faith, not seeing the why of the death of

Jake. In reverse, like Job, I can say that I truly saw God. I saw that Jesus was enough, that He did give me eyes to see past the physical world and know "that the sufferings of this present time are not worth comparing with the glory that is to be revealed to us." (Romans 8:18)

John Piper says that "the deepest need that you and I have in weakness and adversity is not quick relief, but the well-grounded confidence that what is happening to us is part of the greatest purpose of God in the universe[22]."

We will answer God just like Job did: "I know that You can do all things, and that no purpose of yours can be thwarted."[23] When we know this, that our purpose is to see and know God, we move from a place of wanting to know "why" to wanting to know "Who." Jesus. Then we will know that Jesus, without a doubt, is more than enough for anything we might ever encounter.

Yes, it is a fight that must be fought alone; no one can do it for us. We will have to continue wrestling until the break of eternity. We must keep fighting until He shines His final light on

---

[22] http://www.desiringgod.org/resource-library/sermons/christs-power-is-made-perfect-in-weakness

[23] Job 42:2

our dark places. In the end, when our tragedy did not trump us, when we stood firm, and we cried out, "I won't let go until you bless this mess!", not only will we truly see God but others will see God in us.

Yes, I walk with a slight limp now, but I continue walking with Him. Yes, I had heard of Him by the hearing of the ears, but now I *see* God. Now, "I look at the world through tears. But I will see things that dry-eyed I could not see[24]."

Don't stop now; don't give up. When it feels as if the tears have so blurred your vision you can't take another step, keep walking with Him. Keep wrestling.

The dawn is near; the sun is rising, and soon you will see things about Him you could not have possibly seen before. Before too long, you will learn and know that everything you have ever learned about our precious LORD is absolutely true and even more real than you ever knew.

"Weeping may last through the night, but joy comes in the morning." (Psalm 30:5)

---

[24] My paraphrase of Nicholas Wolterstorff "Lament for A Son."

CHAPTER TWENTY TWO
THE POWER OF THE WORD

A few weeks ago, a family in our town experienced a nightmare similar to ours. Their son was killed way too soon. Brad and I knew we needed to go, that they might need us. They wanted Brad to sing his song, "Don't Cry, I Am Home." But as I walked into the church, memories started flooding in.

The church was packed.

Flowers were everywhere.

People were crying.

A casket was open with a child way too small.

My eyes immediately fill with tears; I hurt for them.

I hurt for me.

We entered the sanctuary as Steven Curtis Chapman's song, "With Hope," was playing and I was immediately on edge for this same song was sung at our Jake's funeral.

My first thought: "I am not going to be any help here." Yet, I hugged a mom I have never met but was instantly attached to forever. Circumstances do that. I didn't know her, but I could identify with the tornado she has been tossed into. She looked at me and whispered, "I am going to need you." I simply responded, "I know; we are here."

The only thing I offer to her is a face, a face of a mom who has been where she is and is still standing; and hope. Romans 15:13 "May the God of hope fill you with all joy and peace as you trust in Him, so that you may overflow with hope by the power of the Holy Spirit." My presence offered her a glimmer of hope. We grieve, but we grieve with hope. By the power of the Holy Spirit, we all have overflowing hope. And so I tell God's story through my set of personal circumstances. I wanted you to get a tiny glimpse of what God's Word says because I can offer you a face and hope, but God's Word is the only thing that can heal a hurting soul.

He is the only One who can shed light into your darkest hour. His Word promises that it will not return void and that He will complete the work that he started. He is IT. He is all you need. He is God enough for this.

We will not be like the man in Jeremiah who is cursed for 'drawing his strength from mere flesh and turns his heart away from the Lord.' The woman that 'dwells in the parched places of the desert where no one lives.' But we will be 'blessed because we trusted in the Lord and our confidence was IN THE LORD.' That woman will be 'like a tree planted by the water that sends out roots by the stream. She will not fear when heat comes; her leaves will always be green. She will not worry about the year of drought and never fails to bear fruit[25].'

Let that be said of us. Let it be said that we stood firmly planted by trusting in Him; that regardless of our circumstances, we still bore fruit in Jesus' name. When you are experiencing a drought of your soul, when God's face seems too far or His favor seems to come at too great a cost, know that your leaves can still be green.

Ripe fruit in a desert is far more enticing.

---

[25] Jeremiah 17: 5-8 emphasis and paraphrase mine

CHAPTER TWENTY THREE
BACK TO LIFE. BACK TO REALITY

My husband gave me a week at my parents to finish writing this book. It was the best Christmas present ever. I got most of what I wanted to say on paper.

I left overjoyed at all that had been accomplished. I ate pancakes one last time at my favorite restaurant and then headed home. I was greeted by boys very happy to see their Momma. They were all glad I got to spend a week writing but were also glad for me to be home.

I was also greeted by a dose of reality. Reality slapped me in the face right when I walked through the doors. The laundry was in piles in the middle of the kitchen. The baskets in their rooms were overflowing with dirty clothes.

I cannot even write about what the boys' bathroom looked like. I am still scarred. I was shocked. I just sprayed scrubbing bubbles all over it, walked out, and shut the door. I would enter later with gloves and a face mask.

Why was I so surprised? I have no earthly idea. I knew there would be repercussions from a week away from home. I just wasn't ready for them.

I should have been. It might have had a little something to do with the fact I had been at my parents for a week. I spent a week being spoiled. Coffee and breakfast ready after I had slept in till eight o'clock. My favorite hamburger place (Mooyah's) for lunch each day. No laundry. No fixing food for someone else. No messes. No messy toilets!

Quiet. Peace.

I spent my last few free hours on the the ride home singing and praising the Lord (side note: I sound just like Carrie Underwood in the privacy of my car).

I was on an emotional high after my week spent writing and remembering all that God has done in our lives. I was reminded daily how far He had brought us.

I spent hours reminiscing over His power healing a family. I was full of thankfulness because it is a modern day miracle that we have lived to tell about it. I never even thought about what coming home would be like, I should have gotten a clue when Brad called to ask me about the budget. Budget, PFFT!

Now reality. Today's reality.

It is great to look back and remember what God has done, to relive the awesomeness of where we have been and where we have come. But we must focus on what He is doing now, expecting it to be just as powerful an act as He previously worked.

Yes, my life looks different now – I no longer have to count the minutes since we lost Jake. I live in a different kind of challenge, one that seems so petty in light of past experiences but they are real just the same.

How I long to clean Jake's clothes one more time, yet I curse when the family members I do clean for fill up the laundry bag. How wretched I am!

I know better, yet I still cringe at the dirty toilets and whiny faces. Oswald Chambers says "The true test of persons spiritual life and character is not what he does in the extraordinary moments of life, but what he does during the ordinary times when there is nothing tremendous or exciting happening."

That day I failed in dealing with the ordinary. It is easy to wait for the extraordinary tests in our lives, and we might even pass them. But make no mistake, the everyday, mundane events are just as important and can be just as costly.

Today, you might be counting the minutes, or you may be in the middle of your own nightmare. But we both have a choice in those moments. Will we obey? Will we choose to trust Him when He can't be seen? Will we choose to serve those He has blessed us with?

I can relate to Paul when he says, "I do not understand what I do. For what I want to do I do not do, but what I hate I do. And if I do what I do not want to do, I agree that the law is good. As it is, it is no longer I myself who do it, but it is sin living in me. For I know that good itself does not dwell in me, that is, in my sinful nature. For I have the desire to do what is good, but I cannot carry it out. For I do not do the good I want to do, but the evil I do not want to do—this I keep on doing. Now if I do what I do not want to do, it is no longer I who do it, but it is sin living in me that does it." (Rom. 7)

Mastering my feelings is probably one of the biggest things I struggle with. I don't want to stuff my feelings and act as if they aren't there, but I don't want to vent wrath on those around me either. What is a girl to do?

I have been reading through the Bible in 90 days, and I am amazed at how David talked to his soul. He often asked questions of himself – "Why are you downcast, oh my soul?" (Ps. 42:5) Or he talks to his heart "Be at rest once more, Oh my soul, for the Lord has been good to you." (Ps. 116:7)

It is a Biblical form of self talk. We must learn to talk to our soul – why am I mad about this? Is this really important in the big scheme of things? Am I allowing myself to get worked up over external things?

Yes, there is a righteous anger – usually it happens when someone else is being trampled by others. It is not a righteous anger when I am feeling run over. I am to serve others, not vice versa; yet my anger seems to pop up when others around me aren't doing what I want. I must say to myself "Be at rest, not anger, the Lord has been good to me."

After we lost Jake, this was a battle I had to win. The mind game can be the most costly of battles. Those victories I won back then must still be repeated daily, or I find myself once again bitter or angry over little things. I must learn to talk myself down.

Lamentations three says "Yet this I call to mind and therefore I have hope: Because of the LORD's great love we are not consumed, for his compassions never fail. They are new every morning; great is your faithfulness. I say to myself, The LORD is my portion; therefore I will wait for him."

We have to learn the art of calling to our minds the hope we have in the Lord – not just in the big situations but the small, everyday, mundane issues we deal with. We have hope in the Lord and believe that His mercy is new for us each morning even when I blew it the night before with my kids or my husband.

God is faithful even when we are faithless. God is our portion, meaning He is more than enough for our daily struggles. We must learn to make it a practice to say to ourselves, 'Be at rest, the Lord has been good to you.'

In today's culture I think we have bought into the lie that *busyness equals productivity*. The more we do, the faster we go, the better we are. What happens when I don't stop and walk, or when I am not still before Him? I burn out and want to quit.

One day I am going a hundred miles an hour, and the next day, I can't seem to get off the couch. I haven't learned to live in the middle of the high and lows. I am either too high or too low. I think when tragedy strikes a family, you hit an instant low. God does a miracle in that family, and you hit a high. And back and forth it goes. Up and down.

I have a hard time living in the day to day of life. I keep living waiting for that next high or low to hit. I don't know how to relax. I am anxious for what is up ahead.

I know God can get us through it; I just don't know what we will have to endure to get the next prize. I feel like I am on pins and needles most of the time. The phone rings late at night, my heart skips a beat, dread fills me, and I can't help but think, 'What now?'

My mom will text me and tell me to call her when I have a minute, but she makes sure to tell me that nothing is wrong because I would immediately call and say "What's wrong?". I am still learning that it is okay to walk.

A friend once told me that I live my life out loud. I have always been in a visible position for most of my life. My dad was a pastor as well as on staff at large churches and now my husband is also on staff at a church. There was a part of me that wanted to show off in that role. While growing up, I wanted to show how bad I could be and then as I matured I wanted to show

how GOOD GOD IS. I think in my effort to show others God, I threw myself into a tailspin. I thought I had to single-handedly prove to others how good our God is. I felt a huge responsibility.

    I need to walk, to soak in the normal times. To be still. I need to grasp that God is good, with or without my help.

CHAPTER TWENTY FOUR
MOUNTAIN HIKES AND PRESSING ON

God has left us here to tell His story to others and that I will do. Some days the fact that I am still walking around is proof enough. If we are here, breathing, we have a role to fulfill, a calling to answer. The most important calling of all is to love the Lord your God with all your heart, soul, and mind.

Often, we need walking breaks to be reminded of this. We are called to work and serve (our pastor calls this abounding), but he reminded us last week, we must abide so that we can abound. May we load up on God's Word until we are so full that we spill His love onto those around us.

That is true surrender. That is hard surrender. It didn't come easy, and it wasn't cheap. But the price He paid for us wasn't cheap either. He gave His all, and I want to do the same. I have to give my story back to Him daily and let Him write it. Not me.

I would write into my life ease, comfort, and self gratification. I would write a life that didn't experience loss or pain, a life full of happy moments and tender family time. That is the longing for heaven that God has put into our hearts; we want heaven, on earth. Thankfully in God's plan for my hope and future, He has penned something different.

Learning to live this in the everyday is the hard part; writing about it is easy.

I was speaking at a pastors and wives conference a few years back, and we had free time to pamper ourselves. Many of us chose to get massages. I walked out of my massage feeling glorious.

My friend, however, had mistakenly gotten a deep tissue massage. She walked out of her massage room sore and irritated that her massage had not felt good.

She didn't want a healing deep tissue massage; she wanted to feel glorious like me. The massage therapist told her she would feel better the next day and that it would benefit her in the long run.

We are the same in life. We don't want to feel pain even if that pain is the conduit to our healing. We just want to feel good. Events in our life can feel like a deep tissue massage, as if we have been rubbed raw and beaten. But if you allow God to use that pain, He can use it for your healing.

No, I never discovered why I walked out of the hospital one day with empty arms and another day I walked out side by side with my teenage son.

I don't know why, but I do know WHO. Knowing the WHO is enough. Like my dear friend wrote to me, I just give you Jesus and He is enough.

When you know WHO the why's seem to fade in the distance. Knowing the WHO more deeply is all the really matters any more.

Brad wrote a song that I titled this book after called *God Enough*. It says:

What's that you're carrying? It looks a little heavy to me
Your soul is wearing thin. I just can't let it be
There's something you should know
We gotta learn to let go
Because His arms are...

Big enough, wide enough, strong enough to hold you
He's tough enough, wise enough, strong enough to hold you
He's God enough to hold you. Why don't you let Him?

You've been gone for far too long,
Shouldering the weight of the world
It's time to come back home. He's waiting on your return
There's something you should know
We gotta learn to let go
Because His arms are...

Big enough, wide enough, strong enough to hold you
He's tough enough, wise enough, strong enough to hold you

He's God enough to hold you. Why don't you let Him? [26]

I can't promise you that God will change your circumstances. I can't promise you that He will remove all the pain. I can't promise you that this life will not be full of heartache and pain.

I can't promise you that a life lived to the glory of God will be easy. But I can promise you this - He is God Enough.

He is God enough for whatever circumstance you are encountering. He is God enough to hold you. You just have to decide that you will let Him. Will you please let Him?

I can't promise that when you decide to let Him hold you, the pain will be gone. But I can promise you this - it will be worth it. There will be a day when you will hear the words from your Heavenly Father saying to you "Well done."

On that day, every tear, every heartache, every death, every loss, every "light and momentary troubles are achieving for us an eternal glory that far outweighs them all." I can guarantee you this; the eternal glory will outweigh any heartbreak you encounter. He is God Enough for me, and He will be God enough for you.

---

[26] God Enough by Brad Ewing, © 2011 (see To The Reader section on getting this song for free).

A few weeks ago, our whole family went on a mission trip to Honduras for a week. During the trip we hiked to a remote village that was hours away on a mission to spread God's story of love and grace.

I was not prepared for this type of physical activity. It started out easy and fairly flat. I didn't think I was going to have any problems. I assumed that we would make it to village within the next hour and had no worries for what lay ahead. However, about an hour into the hike, the terrain got steeper and steeper.

I began to get a little nervous.

We got to the top of the first mountain, and I was excited thinking we had made it to the village. At this point, I was told that we were only half way there. I was instantly disappointed because I didn't think I could go anymore. I was already feeling the heat of the sun, the rapid beat of my heart, and overall exhaustion.

When I got to the top of the first mountain, I realized that this hike was a lot like my life. I thought after Drew was born that I had reached the pinnacle of my relationship with the Lord.

Little did I know what lay ahead. I was not even close to the end. Drew's arrival had only gotten my heart pumping for the vigorous climb that was still in front of me.

When I looked out over the peak of the first hill, we were all breathing hard yet encouraged that we could actually see the village named La Gloria that we planned to visit. I could see the end in my sight but had many miles to travel before I reached the goal.

When Jake died, I felt a bit of the same feelings I felt when I conquered that first hill. I thought that I couldn't go on anymore. I was tired and didn't have the strength to carry on. I wanted to quit and pitch my tent right there on the side of the mountain and not go any further.

Brad was with me. I looked at him and told him I couldn't go on anymore. He stopped and prayed with me. He carried my back pack. He walked behind me encouraging me each step of the way. We stopped by a river to cool off. We sat down on a ledge to rest. We finally made it to the top, four and half hours later we reached our destination.

I didn't think I could make it to the village. The village reminded me of heaven. I could imagine what it would be like and knew it to be glorious, but it seemed so far away and the journey was just too hard. I could see the goal in the distance, but the hike was too difficult for me to climb.

Jake's death made me look at eternity and want to be there with Jake and Jesus, but the path to both seemed too hard and long. Looking in the distance, a lifetime without Jake seemed overwhelming.

Just like the day of the hike, I had to look at the life in front of me and just put one foot in front of the other. Often I felt as if I was on a stair climber and not making any progress. But then I would look up and realize that I had made it a few days, then a few months had gone by without my Jake.

Our hike in Honduras is like our life here.

Somedays we have to stop and allow people to pray over us to step another foot.

Somedays our bags are too heavy; we have to have help to take the next step.

Somedays we stop and soak in the Living Water.

Somedays we feel as if we are climbing a Stairmaster going nowhere.

Then one day we look up and realize that we have made it to the top. We look up and realize that yes we are tired and our muscles are sore, but we, with the help of the Lord, persevered through the hardest climb of our lives.

We will one day receive what we have been promised, eternal life with Jesus.

If all of us got what we wanted here on Earth, we wouldn't want heaven. Jake's death took away what I wanted here in this life and forced me to live a different kind of life. A <u>life worth living</u>, a life that focused not on things of this world but on the eternal things. Jake's death made heaven real for me. Jake's death allowed me to see the world through tears, and tears cleared my vision to see God.

My son's death no longer feels like a sacrifice but a privilege. God trusted me to walk through an experience that showed others around us a picture of Jesus. Jake's death opened the door of the gospel to people that might not have heard the message any other way.

I saw Jesus, and suddenly His death on the cross meant so much more. More than my feeble words could explain. In the death of my son, I saw how the death of THE SON changed everything. I could look back and just like Job say, I had heard of God but now I see Him!

Seeing him is worth it all. Jesus is enough for whatever it is that you are dealing with right this minute. Dig in deep with the Lord.

Ask Him your questions; then sit and allow Him to ask you some of His own.

Allow Him to show you who He really is. The "why" of whatever you are facing will fade away when you meet the WHO.

I promise you. He is God enough.

APPENDIX ONE
SURVIVAL PLAYLISTS

Kasey's Top 10 Survival List (Music)

Songs For The Storm (album) by Brad Ewing

Psalms (album) by Shane and Shane

Declaration (album) by Steven Curtis Chapman (especially God is God and Bring It On)

I Will Rise (song) by Chris Tomlin

On The Road to Beautiful (album) by Charlie Hall

I Will Overcome (song) by Charlie Hall

Better Than A Hallelujah (song) by Amy Grant

Blessed Be Your Name (song) by Matt Redman

Beauty Will Rise (album) by Steven Curtis Chapman

One More Day (song) by Lonestar

Revelation Song (song) by Kari Jobe

Kasey's Top 10 Survival List (Books)

1. Bible

2. Job

3. Shattered Dreams By Larry Crab

4. Lament for a Son by Nicholas Wolterstorff

5. When Heaven is Silent by Ron Dunn

6. Heaven by Randy Alcorn

7. Someone I Loved Died by Christine Harder Tangvald (children's book) and Someday Heaven By Larry Libby

8. A Grief Observed by C.S. Lewis

9. My Utmost for His Highest by Oswald Chambers

10. Beth Moore Bible studies

APPENDIX TWO
JOURNAL ENTRIES

I wanted to give you a little deeper inside look of our hearts at the time of Jake's death and after. They are brutally honest and I pray can provide a sense of empathy with one another and trust in the Lord as you go through your own trials.

September 13, 2001

Oh Lord - how it hurts - it hurts so bad. The loss too great. It hurts to think, total denial, who can comprehend such loss? Who can get a grip on this? Images in my head, I can't get them out. They are stained to my memory - I can't get them out. Horrible thoughts - Jake's death, watching him die. What terrible words for a mother to have to say. How does one handle such heartache? Lord, you are the Healer, I need your help. It has been nineteen days since the accident - all I have tried to do is act like it didn't happen and then someone says his precious name and I stop breathing, it literally knocks the breathe out of me.

I am mad. Angry. Not at anyone in particular just mad. If only there was a person who I could unleash my vengeance upon. A person to be mad at. I am not mad at you God. I know enough about your ways to know you are not to blame. I am now thankful for previous trials - trials that taught me you could be trusted no matter what. I just wish it didn't have to be this way. Not my son. I wish he didn't have to die. He was so precious. I know you know that. He is your child too. You could have healed him. I know that you had the power to heal him. Yet, you didn't. I wonder why.

The pain is devastating - I miss him. I miss my old life. I miss my routine, kids schedules, nap times, bedtimes, order. Mostly, I just miss him.

September 14, 2001

"Precious Lord, I've been ignoring my pain and going through the motions. Help set me free. Be the Truth in my life and expose hidden strands of hurt and disappointment. I know I'm not the same person I used to be. Help me to embrace my new identity apart from my loved one. Transform my gray of grief into a new look that lets the truth of my loss and my potential in You shine through. Amen[27]"

What a great prayer - my prayer to you. I needed that prayer, I didn't have the words to express that. I don't even know

---

[27] Kathe Wunnenberg, Grieving the Loss of a Loved One

how to act. Where is the balance of denial and getting through the day? Help me, Lord, to be honest. To grieve. To let your love surround me. Lord, I need an extra dose of you - IV them straight to me. I just hurt all over. My heart hurts. It stings.

Put a guard around our marriage. Don't let us lose what a precious thing we have - Lord, protect our family - put a hedge of protection around us. We desperately need you.

Give us each a heart that can love you more through this. We can't do this alone. We. need. you. now.

September 18, 2001

I thought I heard Jake when I woke up this morning - he was so noisy in the mornings - making whatever sound and noise he could do get us to get him out of his bed. It all feels like a dream, our "old life" so distant and far away. My heart breaks. My soul is dry. Save me, Lord. Comfort me with the comfort only you can give. Help me to grieve. To grieve with hope. I really needed today. To come and do nothing. To be sad, to cry, to run it out on the treadmill.

I thought the days would get easier yet it seems like each one is getting harder and harder. Each day brings the revelation of a new day without Jake. How I miss him, my 'love bug.' I don't know who loved who more - us loving him or him loving us? That smile. He could light up a room. Those curls he had, he was the cutest thing ever. Does he have curls in heaven with you? I hope to see him the same age with curly hair. I miss him. I miss my old life. Be my comfort - my healer. My heart is broken.

September 22, 2001

Oh Lord, some days every second hurts. Some off and on and some are so hard I don't think I will make it for a minute. Then when I have an ounce of relief, I question myself. Am I dealing with Jake's death or denying the pain. How do I live like this? Am I coping or sinking? Lord, I need you. Your strength. Your comfort. You are my all in all.

Jesus, oh Jesus.

The pain of the cross, the torture you went through for me. UNBELIEVABLE, for me?! What a sacrifice.

Lord, I feel the bitterness and resentment rising up inside. I know that it is starting to creep in. How do I remove a root of bitterness. I can feel it spreading inside. Lord, help me to forgive. Help me to show your love. Help me heal. Guard my mouth. Fill me with you and not bitterness and resentment.

I am so mad at everyone - I want them to feel pain like I do. How do I stop and change all these explosive emotions? I want us to be blessings to others and full of love but I don't feel like it. Can you change how I feel? Can you ignite a love for others and not a burning anger. Only you can change those kind of feelings?Will you?

We are broken. Revive us, Lord.

October 1 , 2001

Jake, it's been over a month since you left us. I'm sure (and hope) this is the loneliest month of my life. You are in paradise, but I miss you being with me here. I've been busy at work and haven't had much time to cry; don't think I don't think about you all time. It's just hard to think sad things all the time. Jesus has showed me that I can't come to you yet, so I have a job to let Him do through me. O how I wish he'd just split the sky and we could be together again. I long for that day! My entire heart, body, and soul longs for Jesus' return! But Until Then.

I miss your smile. I miss how you loved people. I miss how you changed lives even at 23 months old. God used you to make me a better man. I wanted to see the man you would become. I am sorry I can't watch you grow up - but I'm glad I don't have to watch you go through any pain. It kills me to think you were in pain at the accident. O how that hurts! Every time! But I know you are with the HEALER now. He will take care of you my son! One Day! One Day! Hopefully one day soon!

I miss your hands. I miss your feet (without shoes). I miss your messes at mealtime. I miss you fits at bath time. I miss chasing you down the hallway and to the couch. I miss watching you say "dance, daddy." I miss you wanting to play with Browning, but not really wanting to - I don't blame you - he's too hyper! I miss hearing you jibber jabber in the mornings! Just happy to be alive! O how I wish I had half your joy. Jake, part of my joy is gone. Tell Jesus to fill me with his completeness now. I really need Him. Tell him for me! Tell him to come and get us and save us! There's a lot I want to say, but I'm tired now. I love you buddy!

Miss you SO much, Daddy

My dearest Jake, oh how I miss you! I wish you were here for Christmas - so excited to see what you would have gotten as presents. I remember you used to pull off all the ornaments on the tree - I remember having to move the breakable ones up so you couldn't reach them. You used to throw everything. How I wish you were here to do that this year.

You were so happy - how I miss your face. Your curls. You could light up a room. I wish I would have spent more time with you - just playing. Just enjoying you. Just being with you - not doing things for you but playing with you. How was I to know that your time here was going to be so short?

You brought such joy to us - I remember laying in the bed and you would pretend you were asleep and then you couldn't help but grin and back up playing again. You were so stinkin' cute. I loved that waddle when you walked with no shoes, which was everywhere. I bet you aren't wearing shoes now in heaven.

Oh, I miss you so much. What I wouldn't give to have you back. I love you Jake. I miss you so much. It hurts so bad to be without you.

Love, Mommy

But Until Then
from Brad Ewing's *Song for the Storm* cd

No one really knows how much we miss you Jake
Although your in heaven now it still hurts
We know your smiling down from inside those pearly gates
Saying don't cry I'm with Jesus now and I'm okay

Well Lord, oh how long till we see
Till we see our son?
And Lord, oh how long will this hurt in our hearts go on?
But until then.

I think I can relate some to how the father felt
When he gave his precious Son for us all
The emptiness a daddy feels when a son has left his side
I can't believe you did that just for us

Well, Lord, oh how long?
Till we see, till we your Son?
And Lord, oh how long
Will this hurt in this world go on?
But until then.

Gonna keep on trusting you
And lean on you like you like we've never leaned before
One day very soon
We'll see our jake again
We'll say son, take us to the one who saw us through.

October 9, 2001

    I can't stop crying. Journal, everyone keeps telling me to journal, its good for you. If I hear those words one more time! Nothing is good for me. It hurts. It all hurts. Truth hurts. Pain is crushing me. Oh God, help me. Take some of the sting away, the burn is too much. Relieve some of the burden. I am so <u>sad.</u> I miss Jake. I miss my life. My house. My routine. I miss my Jake. I can't do it. Oh Lord, I can't. I am tired and weary.

Lindsay had a baby boy tonight. She had a baby boy and I had to bury my baby. Why? Help me. It is a nightmare. Where is Brad? Working late. I need to see him and be with him.

October 16, 2001

2 Corinthians 7:6 "God, who comforts the depressed."

Your word says you comfort the depressed. That would be me. I am depressed. I hurt. I am angry. I am tired - all these wonderful things.

I need you. I need your help. I am hurting, confused, tired.

Fill me up with you, put my focus back on you. I need to readjust. Quiet times, worship times - focus on you. Comfort me - heal me. Wash me - cleanse me.   I need to see some sunshine in our lives- some help here. Direction. Time with you!

October 18, 2001

Ginger, reality is crashing down on me - it hurts so bad. Everywhere I go, everything I do reminds me of Jake. I miss my Jake - I called him my 'love bug.' He brought so much joy to our lives. How do you keep going?

The nights, I almost can't handle them. The sleeping pills don't work fast enough. I hate going to sleep. The darkness and quiet allow too much freedom of my thoughts. They run wild. I don't want to go to bed knowing Jake won't wake me up. Sometimes in the morning I think I hear him and I have to remind myself that he is not here anymore.

I just want my old life back - my routine, my kids, I want normal not pain.

I think of Jake being hit by the car - what must he have been feeling - oh how it must have hurt him - him crying for his daddy - who can live with this playing over and over in their heads. I can't.

We had lived in our house for over a year with no locks on the door - we just walked right in. Over the summer I got this idea that I was going to fix the locks and get a key. It was such a process getting into the house after that - the key was hard to to do. Had I not fixed the lock, Jake might still be here today? Had we just gotten into the house sooner he might not have gone back out to Brad?

Oh Ginger, this hurts so bad. Why won't Jesus save me from this pain, it is overwhelming. I can't bear it. How do I make it?

October 31, 2001

Halloween without Jake. I feel the hurt out there - it is like sometimes I have to keep it at a distance - it is too painful to allow it to get too close. I have to keep it at bay or it will hurt too much. Then I feel it coming regardless, tears fill my eyes. There is no stopping the wave of sadness, no amount of pushing it away. It comes no matter what I do.

Oh Lord, I need you. Your peace. Your comfort. Heal my hurts. Help me get through the night so we can enjoy Halloween. I need to make it through tonight for Drew. He needs to see me without tears constantly filling me eyes. Could you do that for me? One night. Give us relief tonight. I beg you.

December 24, 2001

Merry Christmas, Jake by Brad Ewing

*It's the first Christmas without you, realized that today
and so we walk in sorrow and pray through all the pain.*

*We'll open gifts and laugh out loud with the people that we trust.
Oh how we wish that you were here to share this day with us.*

*The day of joy when Jesus came to set all people free.
To pay the price for all our sin so we could live eternally.*

*So as we're sad that you're not here, this one thing brings us joy
that the very hands that created life, now hold our little boy.*

*So Merry Christmas, baby Jake, we love you very much
and tell the Lord we love him too, and we're thankful for His love.*

December 29, 2001

From Here by Uncle Jon

*We still hear your voice, Lord; we still see your face
But today we can't find our way out of this place
It's darker than normal and filled with more fear
And today we can't see where we're going from here.*

*From here days seem colorless and nights seem too cold
Since you took your child home not yet two years old
With him smiles and hugs and laughs we would find
Now that sweet little voice only sounds in our minds.*

*So here in this place that we wished not to know
Do we struggle to find new directions to go
But it's also here in this mire of sorrow
We know you will fill us with strength for tomorrow.*

*You'll help us remember it was you God who bestowed
This child on our family though nothing you owed*

You allowed us to love him; almost two years of bliss
Though some live their whole lives without one day of this.

So Lord help us rise up and wipe the tears from our face
Make us see what's still with us and give thanks for your grace
Let us know that you love us and that our Jake is still near
For he's in Heaven with you
and that's where we're going from here.

Thank you Jesus for the joy we found in Jake's presence and for your comfort in his absence. May you use his life to open the doors of many hearts for you, Lord.

"Hope!" (Romans 12:12; Romans 8:24-27&38-39)

February 23, 2002

Father, forgive me for my unbelief - for my lack of trust that you have great plans for us - wherever they are. Oh lord, remove the anger and bitterness - let your light shine so that all men may see and know your glory.

I can't believe that Jake has been gone for six months Oh lord, I miss him - give him a hug for me - does he miss me? Can he see us? I know that you are the ultimate parent there is Lord, is there a void in his heart for us? Oh how we miss him - my heart aches inside to see him. There is a hole in my heart - I hope that he is making you smile. So many questions about where he is - what's he doing? Sometimes it hurts so bad I can barely breathe. Thank you Lord for being with me - for bringing me peace - walking with me - keep on carrying me. I need the lift.

I ask that tomorrow Lord, you would fill our hearts with praise for you. Lord, do a work in every persons life who walks through those church doors. Use this opportunity to "restore' our hearts. Bind us to you.

Kasey

August 2011

Dear Jake,

Hey bro! It's been ten very long years without you. I know you are having a blast up there kicking' it with Jesus! By the way, I'm so jealous that you got there before me. More than anything else, I miss you; we all do. There are so many things I miss.

I miss how we used to get every single pillow in the house and pile them all in the middle of the living room and jump off of sofas, chairs, tables right into the middle of the pile. You would get so mad when it was my turn and you would scream "My turn! My turn!" over and over as loudly as you could. It was so much fun. I look back on that now at all of our crazy, awesome memories. It's hard to think about how much fun we used to have and how close we were.

Then you were taken away from me and it was the worst day of my life. I still to this day don't understand why the Lord decided to take you when He did. it took me a very long time to trust in Him and to know that He had the best in mind for my whole family and me.

I am writing this letter mainly to tell you how much of an impact you've had not just on my family but on everyone around us. I know what happened has helped people through struggles that are similar to ours. Not only has it helped other people to grow, but it has helped me as well. I learned to trust Him through anything. I am a stronger Christian now than I would have been had our tragedy not taken place. I'm not saying I agree with your being taken away from us, but I have been changed by it to be the best I can be. No matter how much I miss you each day, I know that one day soon I'll get to see your sweet face again. We will play like old times.

I can't even begin to explain how much I want to see you again and how hard it has been living without you. Well little bro', I can't wait to party it up with you and the King of Kings! I love and miss you more than anything!

Love,

Drew

APPENDIX THREE
THOUGHTS FROM A CLOSE FRIEND, KRYSTAL BURNS

I wanted to give you a perspective from a dear friend who walked this journey with us. I think it will help you if you ever walk side by side a friend walking through a hurtful time. It might also give you a glimpse into how our loss impacted others. When Patrick and I moved to Albuquerque in July of 1999, we were young newlyweds and new Christians who had nothing awaiting us except for the job that moved us there. When we first arrived Patrick was working tons of hours and we were in desperate need of relationships with friends in our same stage of life. We decided we needed to find a church to try to meet some people. We tried out several before we landed on one that seemed to fit perfectly. We loved it because the preaching was very down to earth and practical.

The 2nd week that we attended this church, we went to a greeting area after service where we could meet the pastor. We met the senior pastor as well as the associate pastor. As we were visiting with the associate pastor, he asked us if he could take us and introduce us to some other young couples. They were in the early planning stages of beginning a group for young couples. This was such an answer to prayer because we needed friendships so badly. So he took us to a room where all of these young couples were discussing plans for the new group. That's where we met a couple who would become very influential in our lives. They were then, and they still are even today.

Brad and Kasey had 2 boys – Drew who was 3 at the time and Jake who was just a few months old. I had always loved kids and the Ewing boys were no exception. I fell in love with those kids and that family. Brad and Kasey really took us in and treated us like their own flesh and blood. It was exactly what we needed in that season of our lives. We began to go to bible studies and really get grounded in the word, which was so important for us to mature spiritually. We saw a picture of what true biblical relationships were supposed to look like in our friendship with the Ewing's. We began to go over to their house after church and play cards. Saturday card night turned into almost an everyday thing. There weren't many nights that we didn't spend with our new friends.

We learned about marriage, parenting, and so much more from them. And we LOVED those boys. Patrick and I would fight over who got to feed Jake his midnight bottle. Often times, we would spend the night over at the Ewing's because we had played cards until 2:00 a.m. and we didn't want to drive across town to our house. So, we would sleep on the pull out couch in their living room. We loved getting woken up by Drew every morning. He would wake me up so sweetly and then jump as hard as he could on Patrick to wake him up. Even Patrick couldn't help but laugh all-be-it a quite surprising way to wake up! Then, we would wait for Jake to wake up, and again fight about who was going to get him up and feed him. Those are some of my most fond memories and I will forever cherish them.

  We lived this life with the Ewings for a long time. I even got nicknamed "the nanny" by many people because if Kasey didn't have her kids, I did. And I loved it. I loved getting to pick up Jake from the church nursery. He would hold his sweet chubby little arms out to me and I would scoop him up. I have so many great memories. I remember one day in particular that Patrick and I had stayed at the Ewings. Brad and Kasey had to be up at the church for a big garage sale the church was doing so we stayed with the boys and got them ready. They had left us their Jeep and they had taken our car so that we could have the car seats. Mid morning we were supposed to take the boys to them. So we got the boys ready and started to load them up. But there was one problem – no Jeep keys. We could not find them anywhere. I am pretty sure we were cussing Brad thinking he had taken them. We couldn't get a hold of them (was that before cell phones? Geez, we are old!) so we just began to walk from their house to the church. It really wasn't THAT far so we could totally do it. Well, we had 2 kids –we had never taken 2 kids on a walk, especially that far. It was quite the adventure. Jake was not the lightest little boy in the world. I think Drew had fun – it was like an adventure, but Patrick and I were miserable! We got all the way to the church and were ready to yell at Brad for taking the keys. That's when Patrick reached in his pocket and low and behold – Jeep keys. I was so stinking mad at him. It's pretty comical now, but it certainly wasn't then. I remember staying with the boys a few times so Brad and Kasey could get away for some much needed R&R. We loved it – it was a little like playing house. Except, we didn't have to do any disciplining (I really can't remember the boys ever needing it… seriously, they were angels in our eyes!) and we could take a break anytime we wanted. Although, I would have chosen to be with them any day! I couldn't believe it, but Patrick loved those kids as much as I did! In fact, he is the one who came to me and asked if I was ready to start a family of our own. We had planned to wait about 5 years into marriage, but after spending a year with the Ewing's, we decided we couldn't wait any longer.

I got pregnant with our first son in March of 2001. With that pregnancy I began to feel extremely home sick. I wanted to raise my kids near our parents. We felt like the Lord was calling us home to Amarillo, TX. It was such a bittersweet decision because we had made so many great friends in Albuquerque. God really used that time to grow us up spiritually and otherwise. Albuquerque and the relationships we had there was the best thing we ever could have had for our marriage and spiritual lives. But, we decided to make the move home. It was tough, but we felt it was right. It's great to look back now and see God's hand and how He protected us from a lot of things. Some things had happened with the church and I don't think we would have been able to handle those things very well had we still been there in the middle of it. I think God knew that too. We had matured, but not to the point of being able to handle that situation.

One of the hardest things about our move was being away from the Ewing's. We had spent so much time with them that I felt like I was missing out on so much with them and with the boys. They came to visit us in Amarillo at the end of June 2001. I remember hearing Jake talk and thinking how much I was missing out on seeing them grow up. Sadly, that was the last time I got to see Jake alive. I remember everything like it was yesterday. We all went to eat at Joe's Crab Shack. Jake was eating crackers through the plastic and we were laughing at him. The boys played out on the play set that they had while we attempted to catch up with the Ewing's. Of course, we were interrupted a million times by the kids, but that was okay too. I was just savoring being with them all. I remember Brad changing Jake's diaper on the hood of the Jeep before they loaded up and headed back. If I had known then that was the last time I would see him, I would have savored that last time I held him so much more. But how was I to know?

We got the call in the middle of the afternoon on August 26, 2001. I answered the phone and our good friend Cliff Malone was on the other end of the phone. His voice was shaky and he said, "Krystal, I wanted to call and let you know that Jake has passed away." I was stunned. I could not even stand up and I got so dizzy. My head was spinning. "What did you just say?"

I asked him. Cliff responded, "Jake, he's gone. I knew you would want to know." "What happened? Why?" I asked. "He got run over, Krystal. I'm so sorry." I dropped the phone and Patrick knew something was badly wrong. He held me as I sobbed. He couldn't make out what I was saying. "Jake!" I finally screamed. Through the tears and hysterics I tried to make sense of it all to him. I told him that this had to be a mistake. I picked up the phone to call our friend Lindsay – she would know, she would know if this had really happened. No answer. Patrick called our friend Matt Brogden. He confirmed that what we had heard was true. There you have it, I thought. This is real. He told us bits and pieces of the story. We continued to get calls that night filling us in on more details. We were completely devastated. And we felt so far away. We felt so helpless.

I went into work the next morning and couldn't even make it through my shift. I called Patrick and told him I had to go to Albuquerque. I had to see my friends. I was 6 months pregnant with our son and we really did not have extra money to spend on gas and food for a trip, but I did not care – I needed to go. So we did. We packed up that morning and called some of our friends and told them we were coming. They offered us a place to stay while we were in town. We got there and some other friends of ours were having a prayer meeting for the Ewing's. We decided to go, much to my demise. I didn't want to see or talk to anyone but Brad and Kasey. I didn't want to pray for anyone. I didn't want to "grieve" together. I began to get angry and bitter. I felt like these people were coming out of the woodworks and that they didn't even know the Ewing's like we knew them. All of a sudden they wanted to act like their best friends. I had to work through a lot of anger issues with people who I am sure were well meaning but it was really beginning to wear on me. In my mind, no one could care about that family like we did.

    I felt such loss. I had never in my life experienced those feelings so I was a mess. But I knew I had to pull it together because the next morning we were going to see Brad and Kasey and I needed to be strong. I cried the whole way to the Lowery home. I thought if I could just get it all out I would be ok when I saw them. We pulled up to the house and Brad was outside getting some flowers out of a delivery van. Brad and Patrick embraced for a very long time. I waved and ran in to find Kasey. We used to always give Kasey a hard time because she wasn't your typical girl who would cry at movies or even watch sappy movies really. But I thought okay, here we go. Kasey is going to need me to hold her while she bawls in my arms. Surprisingly she greeted me at the door with a smile. We hugged and I took a double take. She wasn't bawling. I now know that she was taking some things to keep her calm, which is a lot less than I think I would need in that situation. She was pretty entertaining and helped us laugh when all anyone wanted to do was break down.

Then there was Drew. He ran up and hugged me and said, "Are you guys here for Jake's celebration?" My heart crumbled. All this time I had thought about Brad and Kasey and their loss, but I had not even stopped to think of how this would affect sweet little Drew. Oh, those boys were the best of friends. He loved his little brother. How was he going to understand this? We knew that Brad and Kasey had a lot of great friends and family members tending to them. We felt better just seeing them. We felt like a big part of our role in being there was to tend to Drew. We asked if we could get him out of the house for a while. We took him to Chuck E Cheese. Remember, we didn't have kids yet, so at that time Chuck E Cheese was even fun for us. Ha! I remember some of the conversations we had with Drew that day. It was like everything reminded him of Jake. And us too. We saw a little boy that reminded us of Jake. We saw balloons which also reminded us of him. We went to Toys R Us and passed by toy after toy that reminded us of Jake. It was such a sweet day, but also so difficult to try to look at that kind of loss through the eyes of a 5 year old.

That night was the visitation at the funeral home. Patrick had absolutely no desire to go – he did not want to see Jake like that. He wanted to remember him running around, full of life. But for me, it was closure and I knew I needed to go. Patrick was very concerned about me because I was pregnant, but I just knew I would regret it if I didn't see him. So, he stayed back and hung out with Drew while I went with Christy and Lindsay to the funeral home. The minute I walked in I felt the heaviness of what was reality. Jake was gone. Brad and Kasey would have to live forever without him. We were not going to get to see him grow up and find out what kind of kid he would be. I remember going through the line and Brad comforting me. I was supposed to be comforting him, but in that moment he comforted me. I remember seeing Jake, lying in that casket, lifeless. Kasey said to me, "doesn't he look cute?" And he did, but it just wasn't him either. I wanted so badly to just pick him up. To pretend that he was just asleep in the crib and at any minute he would stand up and reach his chubby little arms out to me. But of course, that wasn't going to happen.

We made it through the visitation and the funeral and then we had to go home. Back to reality. Again I remember feeling so helpless. There was absolutely nothing I could do for my friends because I was in Amarillo and they were in Albuquerque. On the way home I remember being struck with fear. I was about to have a child of my own. If something bad could happen to Jake, what if something bad happened to my child? Over the next few months, I read so many books and things to try to manage my grief. I was obsessed with Jake and his death. I talked about him all the time and many of my thoughts were about him and the Ewing family. I have journal entry after journal entry filled with prayers for their family.

In December of that year, we had our first son, Kayden. I was so happy, but so scared at the same time. I now knew what it felt like to love a child, my very own child. I would come up with crazy thoughts about things happening to Kayden. One day it would be that he was going to get kidnapped, and the next day it was that he wouldn't wake up from his nap. I know all moms experience fearing little things about their children, but these fears I had were not normal. They were sick. The enemy was really using Jake's death to torment me. I remember feeling like I had no joy. I remember feeling like God was nowhere to be found.

It wasn't until about 18 months after Jake's death that I really, truly began to experience healing. I heard a sermon that opened my eyes to what I was feeling. The title of that sermon was "Offended at God." Of course! I was offended at God. He took Jake's life and didn't even consider how that would affect everyone who loved him. My friends were good people. They served the Lord with all their hearts. They didn't deserve this to happen to them. I was very angry at God. And He knew it, but I wouldn't admit it. I was saying all the things you're supposed to say to Him in a situation like this – "Lord, I don't understand, but I know you are sovereign and I know your ways are better than ours." What a crock. Deep down I didn't really believe any of that. I was angry. I was hurt. And God was the only one who could have prevented it and He didn't. I can remember sitting in church service after church service and going through the motions. I lifted my hands in worship at all the right times; I closed my eyes so that I was convincing to everyone around me. I prayed, I read my bible and I said all of the proper "Christian" things that we are supposed to say to one another. But, truly, for 18 months, I didn't really worship God. I didn't really have that great of a relationship with Him. I wasn't being honest with Him or myself for that matter.

The night that I heard that sermon, it was as though a veil was lifted. The pastor that preached always had a "how to" at the end of each message – tonight's "how to" was to get real with God. Be honest with Him. So, that night I did. I yelled at Him and told Him exactly how I had been feeling over the last year. He already knew, but the minute I confessed it to Him, I felt Him. And I still didn't understand, and I don't think I ever will. But that night, God touched me. I wrote in my journal that night that I had heard the Lord speak to me and tell me that my heart had hardened. He reminded me of Job and how Job praised God EVEN IN THE HARD TIMES. It says that he tore off his clothes and WORSHIPED. Lord you give and take away, but blessed be your name. Psalm 103 says: "Praise the Lord oh my soul". I had to get myself to a place of praising Him – even when I didn't feel like it…even when I wasn't sure He deserved my praise.

In the difficult circumstance I found myself in, I had to decide to put on the garment of praise to cover my spirit of heaviness. And the more that I chose to put praise on instead of heaviness, the more that God continued to heal me throughout the next several months. The fear that gripped me began to loosen. Never in a million years could I have made it through my grief without His hand. I have a sentence written in a journal entry that says this: "The only guarantee we have in life is that God is good." That's a fact. He's good.

I have learned a lot about this life that we have on the earth and the bottom line is that this life is risky. Very risky. There actually aren't any guarantees in this life. But, because I know who I am and whom I belong to, I know that I am guaranteed an eternity with my heavenly father. And while I look forward to that eternity, I also know that while I am here on this earth, I have a purpose and a destiny. We all do. For a while fear was controlling my life and my destiny. Fear needed to be replaced with trust. Life is tough. Life throws you curve balls and lots of them. I have found in every single hard thing I have experienced in life (some bigger than others) has to do with trusting God. I can say that I trust God all day long, but when the rubber meets the road will my response to any given situation reflect that I truly trust Him? Do I truly trust that He knows what is best for me and that He has my very best interest at heart? Easy to say, tough to live out and it is a daily battle to do so...especially for a control freak such as myself! I have ridden a lot of "roller coasters" in this life and sometimes I want to puke, and other times I have a blast. And sometimes, let me just be honest, I want to get off the stinkin roller coaster and get on a train! A nice slow train ride would just be great every once in a while. At least the operator of any ride I get on is Jesus. Jesus is much easier to trust than a typical carnival ride worker!

    It has been nearly 9 and a half years since Jake died at the time I am writing. I can't believe it. I still think about him. Each August I remember him and the journey that God has brought me through and more importantly the journey He has brought my friends through. And every year on September 9th, I remember Jake's day of birth and the day he was laid to rest. It's funny how a balloon flying in the air can stop me cold in my tracks as I think of Jake. He had this car seat that transferred into a stroller (I had several "fights" with that darn thing!) and recently I saw a mom pulling one out of her car that was just like his. Memories immediately flooded my mind. Anytime I see a curly headed chubby boy, my heart skips a beat. I miss that boy so much.

    I don't know how God carried Brad and Kasey through. I had my own set of issues, but I know that dark time in my life pales in comparison to what they experienced. But, God saw them through…He's still seeing them through. I remember the end of the song that Brad wrote the day that Jake died says "And one day very soon, we'll see our Jake again, and we'll say 'son, take us to the one who saw us through." He was and is enough for them. In the deepest darkest valley of anyone's life – He is enough.

    He's all anyone needs.

TO THE READER

Thank you for reading this book. Our prayer is that you were encouraged to trust the Lord more, or maybe even trust in Jesus as your Savior. We would love to have your feedback.

Go to Kasey's website, **www.kaseyewing.com**, to find her blog, videos, Facebook link, calendar and more. Also learn how to contact her for a speaking event. You can also connect with her at the address on the website.

As a bonus for purchasing this book, please go to the website below to get your free download of my song, God Enough, that partners Kasey's book.

www.bradewing.com/freesong.html

If you were blessed by the book and song, we'd be honored if you'd share it on your social media accounts (Facebook, Twitter, etc.). This is a grass roots, word of mouth sort of deal on our end, so any help you can give would be great. Thanks again for the support of this ministry.

The Ewings

THANK YOU for your support!

There are a few things we want to let you know about.

1. **Don't forget** to download your free song by the same title, God Enough, at **www.bradewing.com/freesong**. (Right-click on the file to download)

2. You can keep in touch with Kasey by signing up for her email list and "liking" her Facebook author page. Both are found at her website, **www.kaseyewing.com**.

We are praying this book will reach many with the love and comfort of Christ. This is a grassroots effort, so we're asking family and friends to help us get the word out.

Here are some ways you can help:
(And there's a gift for those who really get after it).

OPTION 1 - Post comments on your social media (Facebook, Twitter, etc) and provide links to Kasey's website where your friends and family can learn about the book.

OPTION 2 - Submit a review about the book on Kindle, Nook or iTunes.

For anyone who shares a link on social media <u>and</u> writes a review on a book site, we'll give you a free mp3 of an unreleased song called I Promise You (A Soldier's Song), about a military couples' love that will be on Brad's 2012 project.

Please email **info@kaseyewing.com** to inform us that you helped in *both options* and we'll email you the new song.

THANKS AGAIN FOR YOUR SUPPORT!!